Word Crafting

Teaching Spelling, Grades K–6

Cindy Marten

Foreword by Donald H. Graves

Heinemann
Portsmouth, NH

Heinemann
A division of Reed Elsevier Inc.
361 Hanover Street
Portsmouth, NH 03801–3912
www.heinemann.com

Offices and agents throughout the world

The author and publisher wish to thank those who have generously given permission to reprint borrowed material:

"A Speller's Bill of Rights" by Sandra Wilde from *Primary Voices K–6,* November 1996. Copyright © 1996 by the National Council of Teachers of English. Reprinted with permission.

Acknowledgments for borrowed material continue on p. 158.

Library of Congress Cataloging-in-Publication Data
Marten, Cindy.
    Word crafting : teaching spelling, grades K–6 / Cindy Marten ; foreword by Donald H. Graves.
        p. cm.
    ISBN 0-325-00322-X (alk. paper)
    1. English language—Orthography and spelling—Study and teaching (Elementary).   I. Title.

LB1574.M295 2003
372.63'2—dc21   2003014327

Editor: Lois Bridges
Developmental editor: Alan Huisman
Production: Vicki Kasabian
Cover design: Catherine Hawkes, Cat & Mouse Design
Author photograph: Archuletta Ink
Typesetter: Kim Arney Mulcahy
Manufacturing: Steve Bernier

Printed in the United States of America on acid-free paper
07 06 05 04 03 RRD 1 2 3 4 5

To my dear brother,
Charley Cohen,
who has been my inspiration;
not only is Charley an astonishing speller,
he's a courageous learner.
Because of him I became a teacher.

Contents

Foreword

I once asked a publisher why he published spelling texts that ignored everything we know about research in the teaching of spelling. He said, "I give teachers what they are asking for: spelling lists, language arts exercises to keep kids busy Tuesday through Thursday, and a spelling test on Friday. If I try anything else we lose money. Teachers don't really want to think all that much." Indeed, we live in a time when publishers too often give teachers what they think they want and ignore the needs of professionals who want the energy of solid teaching. So many packaged programs related to spelling say to teachers, "Try our method, you won't have to think!"

Word Crafting, refreshingly, is filled with respect for teachers. This is a book for teachers who enjoy the stimulation and energy of helping children think about what they are doing when they spell.

Make no mistake, spelling is important in American culture. In a survey of American parents on the importance of major areas of curriculum, reading was first, mathematics second, and spelling third. Principals and teachers know that if spelling is neglected, parents will be critical. Cindy Marten's book fills an important void in providing lasting spelling power for students.

Cindy has been helping teachers teach spelling for a number of years. Her approach is born of a respect for teachers' ability to take a developmental look at children's emerging abilities to spell. *Word Crafting* contains the details of just how to assess where children are and then shows how to differentiate instruction to help children begin to think about how words are put together. In short, this is an interactive-thinking program that helps children care about words and become lifelong spellers.

The book is filled with resources. Cindy has carefully reviewed the latest in good materials for teaching spelling. In addition, she enlists parents in the process of helping children at home with specific activities that can be done while riding in the car, going to the supermarket, etc.

Cindy's crafting approach to spelling doesn't claim to be a magic potion producing perfect spellers overnight. Quite the contrary, this approach really works, and she has the data to prove it. She shows how her children's spelling grows in proficiency over a five-year period, just the kind of data we'd expect from someone who believes in the craft of teaching spelling.

Donald H. Graves

Acknowledgments

My acknowledgments must start by thanking my brilliant husband Sergio because he has been last for too many years. We met when I was 17, and he has been my number one supporter ever since. He waited for me to finish college and land my first teaching job. His patience while I was in graduate school was remarkable. He brings me hot tea at night as I work into the wee hours. He waits for me to come home from work and return from conferences and never complains about the time away. He makes dinner every night and even does the dishes. He cares for our son in ways that are extraordinary. For once, I am putting Sergio first. He is the first person to thank for this book. He gave me the confidence to try things that I never would have dreamed of trying (like writing this book!). Every person should be as lucky as I am to have a partner who understands and shows unconditional love. This book would not be in your hands without Sergio's caring support.

I've dedicated this book to my brother, Charley Cohen, the best speller I know. Charley is two years older than me and is mentally retarded. The list of what Charley can't do is long and unimportant because the list of what he can do is what matters. His memory and spelling ability are astonishing when you consider that the world of numbers baffle him. Give him any word and he'll spell it correctly the first time. Give him the simplest math problem (5 + 8) and he can't tell you the answer. It is Charley who taught me how to be a teacher. It is Charley who showed me how to love unconditionally and to see the ultimate humanity in every act.

My love of words comes from my dad, and he acquired it from his mother, Minette (my middle name). My father's fascination with words started at a young age leading to his childhood nickname "Dictionary Don." To this day, he does the daily *New York Times* crossword puzzle. He prides himself on doing it backward (starting in the bottom right corner) and in ink. He is genuinely curious and interested in words—a trait we nurture in word crafting classrooms.

My first principal, Jill Green, gave me the courage to trust myself as both a teacher and a learner. She took a huge risk by hiring me fresh out of college to be the new second-grade teacher of a class that included her daughter as well as her best friend's child. Imagine the pressure! Jill showed me every single day how to teach from the heart. I learned what school should be like from her. As a result, it's impossible for me to enter a school without looking for its heart by noticing if teachers treat children and adults with respect.

Another principal, Jeff King, taught me to learn from results and data. His deep commitment to student achievement combined with his "whatever it takes for each child to learn" philosophy left him working tirelessly to remove roadblocks, provide resources, and hire only the best teachers. He knew just when to add a bit of levity to the work that at times seemed impossible. He questioned and challenged nearly every educational trend and mandate that came our way. The transformation and the results achieved at Los Peñasquitos School during my five years working with Jeff were nothing short of a miracle.

I thank my editor Lois Bridges for her deep wisdom and gentle spirit. She brings her heart to her work and helps me keep my voice centered. She has held my hand all the way through this project. And heartfelt thanks to the Heinemann crew who helped realize my dream of publishing a book: Vicki Kasabian, Karen Clausen, and, most especially, Alan Huisman, who saw his way through every page of my manuscript.

One of the first professional books I ever bought was *Transitions* by Regie Routman. My local sales rep, Bill Eastman, politely handed it to me with a "you should try this" look in his eye as if he was selling me a secret. Well he was. And I was hooked. Through my professional reading I have a gained a sense of community and connection that extends far beyond San Diego. It only seems fitting to thank Bill and Pat Eastman at Eastman Educational Associates for keeping me supplied with the best professional books I can find to move my thinking to new levels.

A deep thanks to the teachers at Los Peñasquitos Elementary School who let me work in their classrooms with their students: Carol Adams (word study maven of the school), Lesa Benham, Ruth Fritz, Karon Gentry, Lisa Jones, Beth Lewis, Damen Lopez, Mary Maturo, Pam McPherron, Ed Sandstrom, and Estephanie Ulbert. The rest of the phenomenal teachers in Poway Unified who were my friends and colleagues for six years have contributed to this book in ways that they don't even realize. With my deepest admiration I wish to also thank: Gail Adams, Shirley Day, Janet Malone, Bob Reeves, Jan Gretlin, Sheri DeCremer, Chris DeCremer, Debbie Comer, Pam Coon, Suzanne Moss-High, Stacy Vinge, Sheron Brown, Katie McKinney, and Wendy Smith-Rogers. Each of these colleagues in their special way has helped me grow as a professional committed to continual learning and improvement.

Regie Routman taught me years ago, through *Transitions*, the importance of creating circles of professional colleagues. She inspired me to start a small teacher study group in my living room during my second year of teaching. Then I discovered a larger network of nearly 800 colleagues in San Diego called The San Diego Council of Literacy Professionals. I've been affiliated with this important council for almost 20 years. A deep and sincere thanks goes to my dearest colleagues who have taught me so much over the years: Marianne Barnes, Maureen Begley, Jennie and David Beverage, Linda Chick, Angela Colombini,

Teresa Cubbedge, Bill and Pat Eastman, Lynda Elliott, Barb Hall, Terry Johnson, Carolyn Kalicki, Kathie Kimmy, Marcia Mattson, Mary Milton, Alice Quiocho, Kathy Sibayan, and Judy Sundquist.

At the heart of my work in spelling is what I know about writing. And for that, I thank Lucy Calkins and Donald Graves. I remember having Lucy Calkins' *The Art of Teaching Writing* spread open on my lap like a security blanket when I launched my first writing workshop. Donald Graves showed me how to kneel down next to a child and listen, really listen, for the story that each has to tell. Once you learn to listen, teaching a child how to write is easy. And for research and inspiration about teaching spelling, I thank Louisa Moats and Shane Templeton; I especially appreciate their friendship and kind assistance.

My mom is by my side for every moment that matters. She is my friend, role model, and heroine. Her husband Lee demonstrates his love for family in countless ways. My sister Laura's deep loyalty to family reminds me to take time to be with those we love. My grandma Jane helped by always asking, "When is that book of yours going to be done?" She helped me with the dedication to my brother. My dear friends Danae and Vince Archuletta made sure that the final steps of finishing this book went smoothly by proofreading every page, working on design ideas, babysitting my son for days at a time, and making me laugh when all I wanted to do was cry.

I began my acknowledgments with a tribute to my beloved husband. It's only right I end with a celebration of our darling son, Andrew Marten. Andrew, in innumerable ways, it is you who gave me the encouragement I needed to finish this book. Thank you for keeping yourself busy for hours as I was writing and making me little cards and presents to keep me going. You are certainly the reason I greet each and every day with abundant hope, gratitude, and joy. I love you. Now, let's go on that hike!

Introduction

Learning to spell isn't only about having a good memory. It's about mastering the patterns, principles, and rules that enable us to spell nearly 90 percent of all words in English. Mastery comes with plenty of opportunities to practice and apply those patterns in daily reading and writing.

—Louisa Moats

"Why don't you start next week by teaching spelling? Here's the teacher's manual. And by the way, the student spelling workbooks haven't arrived, so you'll have to figure out how to teach without them." That was how I was offered my first official teaching assignment. It was 1987 and I was a brand-new, wide-eyed student teacher. It was the moment I had been waiting for since I was five years old playing school with my brother and sister.

I clutched the teacher's manual as if it held the secret to turning every child into a National Spelling Bee champion. Surely, I thought, with that manual I would be on my way to producing some of the most proficient spellers east of the Mississippi. I spent the entire weekend reading the script outlined in the manual and planning my first week of teaching. I was panicked that the children didn't have workbooks to do the follow-up lessons, so I coaxed my boyfriend (a better artist than I am) to draw the worksheets for me. First, he looked at the tiny pictures in the teacher's manual (you know, the ones that show reduced versions of the student workbook), then he laboriously re-created a week's worth of worksheets for me. When Monday morning came, I was equipped with enough homemade spelling worksheets to teach thirty second graders the short *a* sound and send them on their way to becoming spelling experts. Ignorance was, of course, bliss. I had no idea how much I needed to know in order to teach a child to spell.

My training in Madeline Hunter's seven-step approach to lesson design required beginning with an "anticipatory set" intended to create *relevance*. This lesson consisted of twenty short *a* words. How, I wondered, was I supposed to make a random list of short *a* words *relevant* to a room full of eight-year-olds whose names I didn't even know yet? So, I just made up random worksheets. I never considered finding out whether the students actually were ready to learn the short *a* sound. That didn't matter. What mattered was that it was the first lesson in the teacher's manual; it was my first teaching assignment, and I was ecstatic to be teaching anything at all.

Looking back, I realize that the teacher's manual was just a security blanket that I could hide behind. Yes, it did tell me *what* I needed to teach, but that's about it. There were some good practice activities in it, but the focus was on *assigning,* not learning. What I really needed was a way to know my students as individual learners—to understand their needs. My focus was on the workbook and *what* to teach. I didn't give much thought to *how* I would teach spelling, *why* I was teaching spelling, or *whom* I was teaching.

I now know that there were many more important questions I should have been asking myself, among them:

- Why is spelling important?
- How do children learn to spell?
- Should I use "content area words," "pattern words," or "high frequency words"?
- Which students are already using short vowels (or any other phoneme) correctly most of the time?

- Which students are using but confusing short vowels (or any other phoneme)?
- Should I have a weekly spelling test?
- What about personal word lists? Are they effective?

Over time, I learned that there is no "silver bullet" in teaching spelling. It is a craft, and many variables influence each decision. A one-size-fits-all answer just isn't enough; it never is. However, there is enough similarity in the development of linguistic knowledge that we don't have to spend countless hours setting up an individual approach to spelling for every student. This book introduces you to some of the components I have found to be critical to effective spelling instruction.

Spend Less Time Teaching Spelling and Get Better Results

This book shows you a simple—yet playful, intellectual, and artful—approach to help you achieve your overarching goal of producing students who can use spelling as a tool for effective communication. It is a departure from traditional approaches because students engage in inquiry and wonder about words.

(An aside here. I'm often asked if this approach will raise spelling scores. My goal was never to find a way to increase spelling scores on a standardized test, yet this approach has achieved exactly that result. Nevertheless, the vastly more important result is that students learn the purpose of spelling and come to understand the linguistic system that helps them contribute to the literate society of which they are a part. Our spelling teaching can be developmentally appropriate, linguistically sound, engaging, and still produce the tangible results that are the public measures of our work.)

In California, where I live, we are required to teach phonics in a way that is "direct, systematic, and explicit"; in response to that "back to phonics" political climate, many well-meaning teachers reach for phonics workbooks. Teachers are being handed so-called teacher-proof materials that promise to "leave no child behind," to make every child able to read, to write, and to spell. States and districts that are hoping to receive No Child Left Behind funding from the federal government must prove that they have put into place scientifically based, research-validated programs.

It is not the place of this book to argue for or against the policies, laws, and programs that are setting the national reading agenda—other books have done an excellent job of exposing the mythology behind such mandates (see, for example, Elaine Garan's fine book *Resisting Reading Mandates*, Richard Allington's *Big Brother and the National Reading Curriculum*, or Gerald Coles' *Reading the Naked Truth*).

Instead, this book is directed to the classroom teacher who is, like me, in the thick of the battle—who shows up every day to teach children and is trying to create a richly literate environment that will nurture lifelong literacy habits. For teachers like us, there simply isn't time for the debate and political strife. However, there is always time to take a closer look at our beliefs and practices in the context of the programs and policies that are being handed to us.

Knowledgeable, informed, reflective teachers know that programs and materials come and go. For example, every seven years we get a new language arts program here in California, and every few years the tests change. Principals come and go, superintendents move on quickly, and school boards have revolving doors leading to power and control. Yes, there are always changes; but the key to remaining firmly rooted during tough political times is to make sure that our own knowledge of children has very deep roots.

What will not change is that twenty to thirty children will show up on the first day of school and you and I will need to teach them—no matter what program is handed to us and mandated, no matter what high-stakes test looms at the end of the year, no matter who sits in power. We just have to remember our first and most important commitment is to our students. Ultimately, we do not work for our principal, our superintendent, our school board, or our politicians; we work for our students. Our work is to ensure that every child becomes an actively literate member of a democratic society who can not only read and write, but who chooses to do so, for multiple purposes and various audiences.

Several years ago, when Sheridan Blau became president of the National Council of Teachers of English, he delivered a moving inaugural speech that underscored what I already knew as a reflective teacher. He honored teachers as professionals when he asserted, "No formula for teaching can be allowed to substitute for a teacher's own professional judgment exercised in the context of a particular classroom, with particular students at a particular moment." The audience burst into applause. He continued, "What we need from school boards and state and federal education agencies is not better models of teaching and learning to be dictated to teachers, but more respect for the professional judgment of classroom teachers and the funds to provide teachers professional development programs that are built on respect of teachers as well as on respect for research, which is to say all professionally honored research. Let us lobby for the right of teachers to practice their profession without the interference of noneducators in matters of curriculum, teaching methods and materials, or research methodologies."

For me, growing professionally over time begins with continuous reflection about the professional books I read, the conferences and presentations I attend, the conversations I share with colleagues, and the work I do with children in classrooms. By investing time in building my own professional knowledge, I have been able to remain focused on what my students need to know. Mandates such as the ones about teaching phonics may cause me to add a new angle to my approach as the materials I'm given begin to change, but what I actually do day in and day out with my students is firmly rooted in my knowledge about how children learn to read and write.

My knowledge is built on the three decades of thoughtful language researchers. I've learned that language is both global and particular. In other words, language that is cohesive and whole is always about communicating and making meaning; but, at the same time, the meaning is conveyed through a particular arrangement of sounds, patterns, and structures, and, in the case of written language, letters, words, and sentences.

I know that in order to learn both the global and particular aspects of language, children need to use language in context, not in isolation. Creating meaning is always central. Trying to separate the particular parts of language (sounds, patterns, and structures) from the global may lead to disconnected learning in which the meaningful nature of language is lost. I have learned to strike a balance that allows students to fine-tune their understanding of language by taking language apart and examining, up close and personal, the pieces that the whole comprises.

I have to admit that I didn't know very much about the particular features of our language system. I spent much of my time studying the challenges children face when they read and write whole texts. I began to study linguistics to learn about the building blocks of our language system. I was not interested in ideological debates, philosophical wrangling, or endless discussions about the reading wars—all of which left me frustrated and brought me no closer to my goal of educating *all* of my students to become actively literate. I simply wanted to learn, and I was especially interested in theories about linguistic development.

Being given mandates and tools to teach phonics was a good impetus to increase my knowledge in this area. I wanted to become a more knowledgeable language educator who could understand how and why these tools and mandates were helpful. I relied on the work of many experts: Louisa Moats, Sandra Wilde, Connie Weaver, Ken and Yetta Goodman, Shane Templeton, Donald Bear, Edmund Henderson, Jo Phenix, Richard Gentry, Patricia Cunningham, Carol and Noam Chomsky, to name a few. As I learned about the developmental stages of my students, I began to understand the linguistic elements of language, and I could see how this knowledge would help me develop more effective practices for teaching spelling.

My hope for you is that your burning questions about *how* to teach spelling will be answered as you look at your own students' spelling, and I hope you are able to make informed and careful decisions about how and when to teach the linguistic elements of our language. When we analyze our own teaching and our own students' learning, we gain insight and build curricular connections that make sense to students, are responsive to standards, and are research based.

Here's what I hope will happen when you read this book: You will come to understand if and when memorization fits into your spelling program. You will build a collection of resources to support your practice. You will equip yourself with the tools you need. You will build your knowledge of the principles for effective spelling instruction to help fill your "tool belt" with strategies. Even more important, you will be equipped with guiding principles that will help you continue on your own.

Several years ago I attended an excellent spelling and word study session at the International Reading Association conference; it showcased concrete examples of children's writing that showed them developing as spellers. While these examples certainly helped us analyze spelling errors, they were dryly written, lacking voice. I leaned over to Regie Routman, with whom I was attending the session, and asked her what she thought. Thanks, Regie, for suggesting, then and there, that I write a book showing teachers how to teach spelling explicitly in the context of real writing. Unless it is accompanied by a strong understanding of how to create a writer, teaching spelling has little purpose. Spelling matters when students have real reasons to write and need conventional spelling to carry their ideas, insights, questions, and inspirations.

Why Spelling Matters

Sometimes spelling is treated as almost a moral issue. I've seen a surprisingly large number of college professors turn livid about student papers with misspelled words, probably more than I've heard them complain about more important matters like lack of authentic voice. But appropriate spelling is really more a matter of etiquette.

—*Sandra Wilde*

Teaching a child to compose thoughtful, clear, well-written work is a complicated process. Creating richly literate classrooms where children engage in meaningful reading and writing activities for multiple purposes and diverse audiences is challenging and vital work. So, where does spelling instruction fit into this landscape of richly literate classrooms? Does it fit at all? If so, how and why?

On August 13, 2000, *Parade* magazine's lead article painted a "good news/bad news" scenario about spelling. The bad news: how you spell makes an instant impression on others. The good news: you can do something about it. The article, written by Marilyn vos Savant (listed in the Guinness Book of Records Hall of Fame for her record IQ score of 228), takes a look at what our spelling says about us.

Earlier, in one of her weekly "Ask Marilyn" columns for *Parade,* vos Savant had included a spelling survey to try to find out whether the ability to spell is a measure of intelligence, education, personality, or desire. A surprising forty-three thousand people responded to her survey, which led her to write a book on the subject, *The Art of Spelling: The Madness and the Method, What Our Spelling Says About Us* (2000).

From this survey, vos Savant drew two major conclusions, both of which offer some insight for teachers:

1. "Excellent spelling ability nearly always indicates high intelligence; however, high intelligence doesn't mainly produce excellent spelling ability. It can produce any kind of spelling."

2. "Low intelligence nearly always produces poor spelling ability; however, poor spelling ability doesn't mainly indicate low intelligence. It can indicate any kind of intelligence."

She also made some simple suggestions about how to improve one's spelling:

- Learn a few rules. Learn some of the basic rules of tricky spelling.
- Look it up. Use a dictionary. Being a good speller is not just dependent on knowing every word. Good spellers know when to look up words they don't know.
- Don't use a spell checker. Instead, write a question mark next to words you don't know how to spell. When you're finished, you can go back and check them.
- Train your motor memory to spell tricky words automatically. Learning to walk or play the piano or sign your name are all connected to your motor memory. By copying tricky words ten times you can train your motor memory to spell the words that cause you the most trouble.
- Pay attention to pronunciation.
- Proofread your work.

Note that these suggestions for improving spelling were made by a columnist, not an educator, and that they are more applicable to an adult who has achieved a basic level of spelling mastery but still has difficulty with "tricky words." Marilyn vos Savant intends to improve the spelling ability of *adults* who have not developed a strong sense of what I call "spelling consciousness." As teachers, our goal is to help our students transcend vos Savant's advice by *teaching* them patterns and principles of spelling while helping them develop their spelling consciousness. Marilyn vos Savant claims that poor spelling in adults is a sign of laziness and is simply a bad habit that can be overcome with proper attention. Her advice to avoid spell-checkers and copy words ten times applies to adults who need to pay closer attention to words they don't know how to spell. Requiring young students to copy words ten times is not a sound strategy for teaching spelling (see Schlagal's [1998] advice on pages 37–38).

Public Spelling Blunders

Vos Savant opens her book, *The Art of Spelling,* with a story about a man who sued a tattoo parlor for $25,000 for a misspelling in his tattoo. The tattoo artist apparently transposed the vowel combination *ai* in the word *villain* so that *villian* was inscribed on the plaintiff's right forearm. Spelling mistakes often have costly consequences, albeit not always with such large penalties. Stories about spelling blunders help show students the importance of developing spelling consciousness.

We know that being a good speller isn't just an academic ability. The more we can show our students that spelling matters for more than the Friday spelling test, the better our results will be. We need to make it clear that poor spelling is almost always seen in our society as a sign of low intelligence, a lack of education, or simple laziness.

As I tell my students, if you are not convinced that spelling matters, consider the following stories. Discussing stories like these helps us become excited about the challenge of learning to spell correctly. Some of these errors have serious financial consequences (like the earlier tattoo story), some are just plain embarrassing, and one even shows us how one misspelling changed a person's identity forever. In each case, a simple spelling error, often committed by a bright and educated person, has far-reaching consequences. All of these mistakes could have been avoided if the offender had developed a strong spelling consciousness early in life.

Road Sign Mishap Not So "Clever"

When a former mayor's name was misspelled on a road sign meant to honor him in Kansas City, Missouri, state transportation workers were undoubtedly red-faced. The city was honoring former Mayor Emanuel Cleaver II by naming a street after him. The local paper reported that the "not so clever" state employees posted signs showing the former mayor's name as "Clever." Dozens of calls flooded into the department of transportation offices as soon as the signs were posted. Isn't it curious how many people noticed the misspelling after it was already up? What happened to the people who ordered the signs, received the signs, and posted the signs? How did the mistake get by so many people? Fortunately, the former mayor was not insulted by the misspelling. He was quoted in the local paper as saying "Everybody's noticed it except for the people who put the sign up. It's not that big of a deal to me. I am an atrocious speller myself so I have great sympathy for people who get caught misspelling something."

Maybe Tomorrow, Prime Minister Blair

When Britain's Prime Minister Tony Blair was caught misspelling the word *tomorrow* three times in a handwritten note to a political colleague, it made headline news with the BBC (see http://news.bbc.co.uk/1/hi /uk_politics/1668516.stm). Here is the text of the infamous note:

> This is just a note to wish you luck toomorrow. Best of luck to you and, of course to Ipswich Town in toomorrow's big game. I'm sure Inter won't be relishing this after Ipswich's superb performances in the last two rounds. I hope there are two good results for Ipswich toomorrow.

After the news broke, the secretary of education jumped on the publicity bandwagon: "It looks as though the government's so-called commitment to life-long learning needs reinforcing at the top. As a symbol of promises in education not being matched by performance, this is impossible to beat."

What better example of the serious consequences of an undeveloped spelling consciousness! These errors could have easily been caught if Blair had simply taken the time to check the words that he knows always cause him trouble (something I always teach as part of developing spell-ing consciousness). At least he did the only proper thing to do when you make a spelling mistake. He owned up to it plain and simple, admitting publicly that *tomorrow* is a word that he has difficulty spelling. He very honestly admitted, "I gather there was what can only be described as a very lame attempt by my press office to suggest it was just my writing and not my spelling. I regret I will have to put my hands up fully and say no it was indeed my spelling that was at fault."

The press even went so far as to find Blair's former English teacher, who (it is fascinating to see), had recognized this pattern years earlier: "The future Prime Minister always had trouble spelling 'tomorrow,' even thirty years ago. If I told him once I must have told him a thousand times."

President Clinton Announces "America Roads" Literacy Project

I received a letter promoting Clinton's "America Roads" initiative. Before you start imagining that the America Roads Literacy Project is a plan to create drive-thru bookstores and libraries (which might not be a bad idea), take a look at the consequences of that one little slip of a vowel from *e* to *o*. Needless to say, if the company producing this expensive report can't even spell the word *reads*, I am not interested in buying their report. I use their letter as an example of spelling's social consequences. It makes a perfect launching point for the unit called "Developing Spelling Consciousness" that I created for fourth or fifth graders (for more on spelling consciousness, see Chapter 4).

What's in a Name?

Here's another story that shows my students spelling consequences. Dionne Warrick's official music industry career had just kicked off when copy editors made a tiny mistake that had giant consequences for her life. The slip of just one letter on her record label caused the budding young musician to change her name permanently. We all know her as Dionne *Warwick,* but her real last name was *Warrick.* In 1962, her life was changed forever by that crucial spelling error on the label of her debut album, ironically titled, "Don't Make Me Over."

Spelling Accountability

In a mistake even more embarrassing than Tony Blair's, Massachusetts State Treasurer Shannon O'Brien decided to rise to the challenge made by another politician when he announced during a debate, "Most city politicians are so out of touch with voters they don't even know how to spell the word *accountability.*" O'Brien accepted the challenge and promptly misspelled the word by leaving out the second *i.* After admitting her mistake, she said, "I am so embarrassed. I just hope that my sixth-grade teacher doesn't read about this, because I was a star speller in his class." O'Brien, a Yale graduate, also added, "I do know how to spell *accountability.* I was so busy thinking of the joke I was going to make after that I wasn't thinking of the spelling and missed it."

Dicing Potatoes

Of course, one of the most famous public spelling mistakes of all is then Vice President Dan Quayle's *potatoe* catastrophe; but if you thought his "dicing" of that word was his worst mistake, there are others. As the 1989 Quayle family Christmas card shows, Quayle is no stranger to embarrassing spelling mistakes. The family joyfully sent this holiday wish to all on their Christmas list: "May our nation continue to be the beakon of hope to the world."

Developing Spelling Consciousness in the Classroom

Arguably one of the most overlooked parts of an effective approach to teaching spelling is developing spelling consciousness. When we, as teachers, find ways to ignite our own authentic enthusiasm and awareness about words, we show our students how to develop an interest in words and spelling. Students then start to pay attention to words and begin to realize that when words are misspelled there are social consequences ranging from miscommunication to embarrassment to financial obligation. Creating spelling consciousness is more than just teaching students to find all the misspelled words. It's a much more dynamic process that also leads them to explore the social consequences of misspelling.

The examples above demonstrate how even the simplest spelling mistake can alter the meaning and importance of the subject. As a society, we tend to place those who make spelling errors into the uneducated category. Not only that, misspelled words reduce anyone's chance of being understood or considered intelligent, and they are an annoying nuisance to others. When I receive an important document that contains misspelled words, I feel as if the author did not put much effort into her or his writing. That may not necessarily be the case, but first impressions make lasting impressions, as I often remind my students.

With the preceding stories as examples, you can begin your own collection of spelling blunders. Just being on the lookout for misspelled signs around town is a perfect way to develop an attentiveness to spelling. Your students can snap photos of the misspelled signs or bring in the offending printed material and add them to a class album of spelling blunders. You'll be surprised how many they find!

An interesting discussion will likely ensue as students come back with signs that are misspelled on purpose (like Krispy Kreme). Having students list name brands that are misspelled on purpose is a great little exercise. You will be surprised at how many companies purposely misspell product names.

Ultimately, you will not want your main message about spelling to be one of "it's important to be a good speller so that you don't look uneducated." This is a reality and can be part of your message and your approach. However, it's more important to remember that when we care about what we are writing and about who is going to read it, our spelling improves considerably. Certainly developing spelling consciousness is helpful and important, but the best way to develop it is to make sure that students are writing for real purposes and audiences. When the writing really matters, the spelling is better.

Teaching Spelling as a Craft

I can learn through the order of experiences contained in a craft if I am willing not to be hasty in drawing conclusions and if I am willing not to think I know better and can manipulate the order of experiences. The craft will lead me if I am able to put aside my impatience and follow.

—*Carla Needleman*

Craft and the Order of Experiences

As teachers, our approach to spelling instruction is often quite hasty. With so many pressures and demands on our time, we search for easy answers and prepackaged programs, hoping to find just the right tool that is quick and easy. We don't have time to write our own spelling curriculum. The good news is we don't have to write our own curriculum or spend lots of time and money; we simply need to increase our knowledge about how spelling develops and get smarter about how to teach spelling in the contexts of what we are already doing.

By approaching spelling instruction as a craft in which we learn how to work with words in the same way that a woodworker learns to work with wood, we will discover what Carla Needleman (1993) calls the "order of experiences contained in the craft." If we, as teachers, invest the time to learn how spelling develops, we will be able to use that knowledge to take a more reasoned and thoughtful approach to spelling instruction that takes less time and gets better results using the tools we already have. We will then help our students enjoy learning how to spell and understand why spelling matters.

Mastering the art of teaching spelling takes time. If I woke up today and decided to be a wood craftsperson, I would be in trouble. I have no idea how to build something like a table. Where would I start? What would my first step be? Wouldn't it be a mistake to try to build my knowledge of the craft by going out and buying a bunch of tools? I would have no idea which tools to buy. That is not to say that I won't need some tools at some point; but in the natural order of experiences, my first step shouldn't be to spend a lot of money on tools.

The same idea holds true for becoming a "word-crafting" (or spelling) teacher. If you start by buying a bunch of word-study tools (workbooks, computer games, spelling games, phonics flash cards, or test preparation materials), you will bypass many of the experiences that help you know which tools you need and how to use them. When you go shopping too soon, you run the risk of wasting your money and your time; and, even more important, you may waste your students' time with unnecessary projects and activities.

So, if buying tools is not the correct first step, what is? How do we, as teachers, begin to learn about our craft? What is the natural order of experiences that will lead us to a deeper understanding of our craft? Well, I know that if I wanted to learn the craft of fine woodworking, I would probably go to my neighbor's house first. He is an expert wood-crafter and he builds beautiful custom-made furniture. My neighbor's first reaction to my slightly nutty idea might be just to send me to a furniture store to buy a table. But if I convinced him that I truly wanted to learn and understand the craft, he would then probably have me start by learning about all the different types of wood. I would learn all about their unique features, textures, and aging patterns. In the same way, when you are becoming a word-crafting teacher, the first step is to learn all about your students and their knowledge of spelling. Spend time watching them write, and then analyze their spelling abilities so that you can gain some insight into their stages of development. Develop a curiosity about how children learn to spell that will cause you to pay attention to the way they spell.

Analyzing spelling errors is an intriguing puzzle, and in solving it you learn what to expect to see. You learn that words are not just spelled two ways, right or wrong, but that in fact there are very predictable and logical ways students misspell words. Once you learn that all children pass through stages of spelling development, you will want to know where your students' spelling falls on this continuum. You will never look at a misspelled word the same way again. Rather than marking a word wrong with a red pen, you will understand the error as part of an evolving system of understanding how to spell.

The stages that students pass through are widely recognized by researchers. Generally, the names for these stages are: prephonemic, letter name, within-word pattern, syllable juncture, and derivational relations. (Different authors call these stages different names. I've used the terms introduced by Edmund Henderson, at the University of Virginia. Interestingly, some of the leading experts in word study today were Henderson's students, among them Shane Templeton, Donald Bear, Richard Gentry, Jerry Zutell, Marcia Invernizzi, Darrell Morris, and Robert Schlagal. Each of these researchers has slightly different names for the stages, but the concept is the same.)

Analyzing students' spelling errors is very much like analyzing miscues in reading assessment; the difference is that in spelling we are analyzing miscues in relation to "encoding" instead of "decoding." Paying attention to the way students spell (strategies they use, linguistic features they apply correctly, high frequency words they know) and understanding how their spelling attempts (miscues, or invented spellings) fit into a broader context of spelling development is the first step in becoming a word-crafting teacher. This takes time. As Needleman points out, when you are learning a new craft, you must resist the urge to skip or manipulate the natural sequence of steps.

Imagine an experienced craftsperson working in her woodworking shop. She has built all kinds of custom-made furniture, including desks, chairs, and bookshelves. She's built hundreds of beautiful pieces. Sometimes her furniture finds its way into small apartments and sometimes into mansions; but certain aspects of the work are always the same. The same material, the same tools, and the same degree of craft go into the construction of every well-made piece of furniture. Whatever she makes, she knows that she will probably need a hammer, nails, glue, and sanding equipment. She has expertly equipped her workshop with the exact tools she needs, and she has spent years adding to her collection. She uses some tools every day; some she rarely touches. She knows exactly which tools are hanging on her tool wall or buried in her tool chest and which of them are highly specialized and might not be needed for every job. She carefully selects the appropriate tool at the precise moment it is needed to accomplish the task at hand.

Now, imagine a novice woodworker. He is full of energy and enthusiasm for his work. In his zealousness to prepare, he has set up shop with every top-of-the-line tool he can find. He has even more tools than our veteran craftsperson, and his are new and fancy. His shop is perfect. So, what's missing? The answer is craft and experience. Those two things cannot be purchased in a catalog. They come only from years of hands-on work.

Teachers are typically given only one tool, if any, to teach spelling, usually a published program that either stands alone or is embedded in a language arts curriculum. However, if my woodworking mentor tried to give me only one tool with which to build my first table, I would never be able to build it. The same is true for the word-crafting teacher: the tools we use are largely determined by the students' stage of spelling development. There are, of course, some basic tools that work no matter what, and others that are used only for special purposes (see Chapter 5 for guidelines about selecting specific tools). As you become a word-crafting teacher, you will gradually collect your tools, item by item, until you have a toolbelt full them—each one carefully selected for your students.

The next step in becoming a word-crafting teacher is to ask yourself what you want your students to know about words, and why spelling and word knowledge are important. Traditional spelling instruction is more a rote routine than an engaging craft. The focus is on memorization, the word lists, the lessons, and the spelling tests; but the students' developmental needs are not addressed. Those traditional approaches are based on a static "scope and sequence" outlined by a textbook divorced from students' needs, and they may not correspond to developmental stages.

As teachers who were trained in the traditional way, we may not even realize that our teaching is more focused on the tools and the curriculum than it is on the students. Since we can err on the side of being too closely focused on the child and run the risk of ignoring the curriculum, or err on the side of focusing too closely on the curriculum and run the risk of ignoring the child, we need to balance them out. By using multiple measures that give us continuous feedback (both formal and informal), we are now able to create a system—word crafting—in which the *art* and the *science* of teaching spelling blend naturally.

Another important step in the process of becoming a word-crafting teacher is to develop your own list of "essential practices." Teaching spelling as a *craft* is as different from traditional approaches to spelling instruction as purchasing a pressboard bookshelf is from building one from scratch. The practices for the prefab bookshelf are simply: buy it, use it. Practices in traditional spelling approaches are much the same: buy it (the program), assign it. Chapter 4 addresses the essential practices of a word-crafting classroom.

Because of the expertise that goes into their work, something made by an artisan is usually considered beautiful and valuable. A beautiful handmade walnut bookshelf, designed and built with the utmost care and skill, is more desirable than a pressboard bookshelf put together with a screwdriver in twenty minutes. I feel the same way about spelling. Sure, there are plenty of quick and easy ways to teach spelling: tricks, techniques, programs, worksheets, and ready-made activities. Students may learn isolated words when they memorize them for spelling tests, but their word knowledge is much stronger when they have first investigated words and studied how words work. I prefer to design my approach to word study as a craft that entails the use of multiple tools and deeper levels of engagement.

One of the key elements of word crafting is that we work to create meaningful contexts in our classrooms that help our students become intrigued by words. Yes, we are looking at individual letter sounds and word patterns, but we are doing it in a spirit of engagement and inquiry. We are excited about the fine points, the particular linguistic elements of language, just as we were excited about using real, high-quality children's literature instead of the basal reading series. In a word-crafting approach, the excitement of learning language drives the work as students and teachers learn and explore words. Together, we play with language and enjoy finding patterns, using suffixes, prefixes, and Latin or Greek roots. We develop an inquisitive stance, looking reflectively at language with our students. At the same time, we are carefully orchestrating and designing lessons and word activities that are appropriate to our students' developmental stages.

So Many Methods—Which One Is Best?

In an examination of the history of spelling instruction Schlagal (1998) points out that, "In recent years, there has been considerable controversy regarding the best way to teach spelling. Some educators favor the use of traditional spelling books featuring the weekly spelling list (Templeton 1991). This position maintains that English spelling is learned developmentally through formal study of some three thousand words across grades 2 through 8, emphasizing that the internalization of these words and the patterns they represent provides an important foundation for spelling and reading the English orthography (Chomsky and Halle 1968; Henderson 1981; Schlagal 1992). In this framework, spelling textbooks offer the teacher an organization of developmentally appropriate word patterns for students to learn at each level." Many of these same educators claim that the best results are achieved when spelling patterns are taught at a student's instructional level (Beers and Henderson 1977; Henderson 1990; Bear, Invernizzi, Templeton, and Johnston 1999; Morris, Nelson, and Perney 1986; Schlagal 1989). There are some who argue that teachers can use spelling textbooks and weekly spelling tests purposefully to teach patterns at a child's instructional level.

In the same article Schlagal describes how "Other educators argue that arbitrary list learning should be abandoned and that spelling instruction should be integrated with other subject areas" (Wilde 1990). "[They argue] that a spelling curriculum is unnecessary (and undesirable) because a teacher can best facilitate spelling development through rich, varied writing opportunities where spelling errors can be responded to as they come up" (Bean and Bouffler 1987; Wilde 1990, 1992). Perhaps simply giving students frequent and extensive exposure to printed material, along with many opportunities to read, allows them to internalize spelling words and patterns. There is some evidence that children learn spelling patterns by reading and rereading their favorite stories. Some educators assert that spelling doesn't need to be taught at all and that reading impacts spelling development more than any other activity (Moustafa 1996; Krashen 1991).

Still another approach emphasizes the memorization of high frequency words (Sitton 1996). Words are assigned, memorized, and tested until a child knows them. In this approach, the weekly list in the text-book may not be presented in a developmentally appropriate sequence. The lists might be thematic or based on frequency, rather than a clear linguistic pattern to explore. Spelling textbooks, in this case, are used in a traditional five-day pattern with a Friday test.

Some educators argue that you really can't teach spelling—either a child is a good speller or he is not. As one teacher explained it to me, it is of no use to teach spelling, because either a child has "the spelling gene" or he hasn't. She asserted that a child's ability to spell is purely based on genetics and consequently she refused to teach spelling at all.

So, which theory or approach is right? It depends. Before you begin to side with one theory or another—see Schlagal (1998) for a more comprehensive summary of the various approaches—and before you commit to a single methodology, decide what you yourself believe about spelling and what your state's standards expect your students to know by the end of the year. Think about why you teach spelling, and then begin to make some decisions about how you will meet your students' instructional needs. In a word-crafting classroom there is room for all three approaches: smart use of a traditional workbook (if you have to use one) in the spirit of inquiry and social learning; memorization of certain frequently misspelled words; and, most importantly, plenty of opportunities to read and write.

Effective Spelling Instruction— Making the Paradigm Shift

In 1999, my school district, Poway Unified, was given an opportunity to evaluate the effectiveness of spelling instruction in its schools. The decision to take a close look at our spelling practices was driven by the superintendent's disappointment over the relatively poor scores our district received on the state's standardized test in spelling. Teachers were also becoming increasingly frustrated with the poor results and lack of a cohesive spelling curriculum. Those scores, combined with an interim statewide adoption cycle that included many new spelling programs, led to the formation of a districtwide spelling leadership team and task force. Ordinarily, I wouldn't be interested in serving on such a committee. But Janet Malone, one of our district administrators, made this much more than a group of teachers rubber-stamping a workbook. She designed a three-year process that included time for us to do the in-depth work of redefining spelling instruction. Thanks to her vision and leadership, we were able to approach our work in spelling reform from a developmental point of view, the approach I had been applying in my third-grade classroom and then as a site-based reading specialist. I worked in several classrooms modeling the approach. Here was a perfect opportunity to share what we had learned at our school with the entire district.

Our district spelling steering committee was made up of five classroom teachers representing primary, elementary, and middle school. It was clear to us from the start that our current approach was limited because it was based completely and exclusively on memorizing high frequency words. We didn't necessarily disagree with memorization as one way to build spelling knowledge; we just knew it wasn't enough. We had only one tool in our spelling toolbelts—"the drill." We drilled the students week in and week out until they had memorized the assigned word lists.

Our steering committee decided to work first on defining the "principles of effective spelling instruction" to make sure that everyone was on the same page. We knew that if we looked at broad research we would be able to define a comprehensive, cohesive approach to teaching spelling effectively in our district.

The Big Ideas About Teaching and Learning Spelling

We then identified a larger team of teachers (two from every school in our district) and read and synthesized six key articles. It was by no means an exhaustive list. For every article we read there were ten more we would have liked to use, but we had to narrow our choices. This is a summary of what we learned:

1. "Questions Teachers Ask About Spelling," by Shane Templeton and Darrell Morris, *Reading Research Quarterly,* vol. 34, no. 1 (January/February/March, 1999), pp. 102–12.

   - Spelling instruction needs to be developmentally appropriate.
   - Exploring the patterns of language is essential.
   - Patterns fall into three categories: sound, structure, and meaning.
   - Spelling knowledge drives reading and writing.
   - Older students should work with derivations.
   - Patterns can be generalized to discover rules.
   - Rules are learned through:
     - Word sorts.
     - Games.
     - Word building.
     - Word-study notebooks.

2. "The Timing and Teaching of Word Families," by Francine Johnston, *The Reading Teacher,* vol. 53, no. 1 (1999), pp. 64–75.

   - Research supports the usefulness of word study.
   - Rimes are the basic units for reading, and for spelling words by analogy. (Rimes like: _ot, _ag, _op)
   - Children are more successful at breaking apart the onset and rime in a word than they are in breaking apart individual phonemes.
   - Phonics is influenced by regional dialects.

- Teachers should use students' "invented spelling" to understand their developmental levels.

3. "The Integral Character of Spelling: Teaching Strategies for Multiple Purposes," by Robert Schlagal and Joy Harris Schlagal, *Language Arts,* vol. 69 (1992), pp. 418–24.

   - Children need to be placed in spelling programs designed for their instructional levels.
   - Working on the structure of words has a positive impact on spelling and reading.
   - English spelling is principled and ordered, and students' errors reveal their developmental stages.

4. "Three Paradigms of Spelling Instruction in Grades 3–6," by B. G. Heald-Taylor, *The Reading Teacher,* vol. 51 (1998), pp. 404–13.

   - Traditional paradigm:
     - Spelling instruction is based on attitudes and practices rather than on research.
     - Spelling is a separate subject rather than the bedrock of literacy.
     - Teachers are "givers of information."
     - Rote phonics addresses 46 percent of words.
     - Strong visual spellers could spell equally well (without formal instruction) if reading/writing were emphasized.
   - Transitional paradigm:
     - Integration of spelling strategies is important.
     - Reading matters and it should be interactive.
     - Students should study words that come from their reading.
     - Words need to be grouped according to a clear orthographic principle.
   - Developmental paradigm:
     - Students are actively involved in word study.
     - The spelling knowledge employed by students follows a clear developmental continuum.

- Reading provides the content.
- Writing has a functional component and needs to communicate meaning.
- When separated from writing, spelling serves no purpose!

5. "Principles and Practices," Chapter 2 in *Spelling K–8*, by Diane Snowball and Faye Bolton (Stenhouse 1999), pp. 5–16.

- One of the goals for student writing is for other people to be able to read and understand it.
- Writing is valued even if the spelling *isn't* all correct.
- Students develop an interest in words and spelling.
- Spelling includes knowledge of how to apply phonics, patterns, and meaning.
- Students learn to develop hypotheses about patterns.
- Students learn high frequency words.
- Students learn how to use a variety of resources when they don't know how to spell a word.
- Reading, writing, and spelling are all seen as connected.
- Developmental stages are taken into consideration.

6. "Multilevel Word Study: Word Charts, Word Walls, and Word Sorts," by Dorothy P. Hall and Patricia Cunningham, Chapter 10 in *Voices on Word Matters: Learning About Phonics and Spelling in the Literacy Classroom,* edited by Irene C. Fountas and Gay Su Pinnell (Heinemann 1999), pp. 114–30.

- Spelling is developmental.
- Classes should have three different groups.
- Whole-class activities should be multilevel.
- Activities should:
  - Involve both the teacher and students (teach, don't assign).
  - Be hands-on.
  - Have something for everyone.
  - Be enjoyable.

- Make connections:
  - By transferring spelling patterns to unknown words.
  - Using word hunts (looking for words in reading and transferring them to wall charts categorized by sound or pattern).
- Introduce multilevel activities:
  - Word charts.
  - Making words.
  - Word walls.
  - Word sorts.

Having synthesized some research about spelling instruction, we then worked as a team to identify the characteristics of a proficient speller. A proficient speller is one who:

- Values spelling as a foundational tool for effective written communication.
- Understands the orthography of English—how words are formed based on sounds, patterns, and meaning.
- Is strategic—knows what to do when attempting to spell an unfamiliar word or when recognizing and correcting a misspelled word.
- Applies spelling knowledge and strategies to all written work, *not* just a weekly test.
- Has developed a spelling consciousness and cares about work being spelled correctly.
- Views word study as fun.

Finally, we made the following list of the seven components we believed to be essential for teaching spelling effectively:

1. Formal and informal assessments are used on an ongoing basis to determine each student's developmental level.

2. Instructional time is planned to provide regular opportunities to meet each student's individual needs.

3. The classroom context includes extended time each day for authentic reading and writing.

4. Students learn to generalize spelling sounds, patterns, meanings, and rules.

5. Students learn strategies for memorizing high frequency words identified by the district/school as appropriate for their grade level.

6. Instruction encourages active participation.

7. Student progress is monitored through ongoing assessment.

Thus we laid the foundation for our philosophical shift from the idea that merely assigning word lists is an adequate way to teach spelling to the idea that teaching spelling is a craft that involves specific components addressing Sandra Wilde's "A Speller's Bill of Rights" (*Primary Voices K–6,* November 1996):

The right to express yourself in first-draft writing regardless of what words you do and don't know how to spell.

The right to do a lot of reading, which is probably the greatest single factor in spelling acquisition.

The right to actively construct knowledge about the spelling system.

The right to learn that spelling does matter.

The right to a developmentally appropriate education in spelling.

The right to know about and have available a lot of ways to come up with spellings (including just knowing how to spell the word).

The right to learn how to proofread.

The right to have spelling placed in its proper context as a small piece of the writing- and language-learning process.

The right to be valued as a human being regardless of your spelling.

Finding a Program

Since we had no formal spelling program, all of us who taught spelling were eager to adopt a published program. We couldn't wait to get a "real program," and publishers were, of course, eager to provide us with one. However, since we were so desperate for help, we were concerned that almost *any* published program would look good to us, compared to what we had (which was nothing except our district-developed high frequency spelling word lists and activities).

In order to simply not take the first program we found, we set about carefully selecting our own criteria; we then developed an evaluation form with a list of criteria for effective programs (see Appendix A). This tool gave us an important lens through which to evaluate the published programs and select the one that would best support our components of effective spelling instruction. We rated seven programs and eliminated five of them right off the bat, and neither of the two remaining met all our criteria. Finally, after an extended pilot and feedback process, we selected Houghton Mifflin's Spelling and Vocabulary series. We especially liked that the word lists were developmentally based and followed an appropriate sequence. Some of the other programs had word lists that were based on themes or on high frequency words, but they were not presented in a clear developmental sequence.

Because we wanted to provide the teachers in our district with a clear continuum for becoming more effective spelling teachers, we created a self-evaluation matrix, Innovation Configuration for Effective Spelling Instruction (see Appendix B), based on our seven components of effective spelling instruction. (The prototype for this matrix, a very useful tool, was developed at the University of Texas at Austin in the Research and Development Center for Teacher Education and brought to us by Janet Malone.) From this matrix, we developed hypothetical case studies of teachers at different places on the continuum as a way to clarify and communicate our expectations related to the principles of spelling instruction (see Appendix C).

The Results

After three years of support for more effective spelling instruction in the district, our efforts were reflected in our improved standardized test scores (see Figures 2–1 and 2–2). One of the most important things we learned was that if you want your spelling scores on the mandated, high-stakes, norm-referenced tests to go up, you must resist the urge to make your students complete endless test-prep sheets. Having a child look at misspelled words and "bubble in" correct answers on a test form does nothing to make him or her a better speller. At best, these tedious activities are test practice, but they certainly do not engage students in actively learning about spelling patterns and principles.

District Results

	1998	1999	2000	2001	2002
Second Grade	64	67	71	76	76
Third Grade	61	66	69	73	75
Fourth Grade	69	69	75	77	79
Fifth Grade	65	65	66	73	74

Results at Los Peñasquitos School

	1998	1999	2000	2001	2002
Second Grade	54	62	71	78	77
Third Grade	51	67	70	71	76
Fourth Grade	55	56	68	76	81
Fifth Grade	52	53	57	57	69

Figure 2–1. SAT-9 Spelling National Percentile Ranking, Poway Unified School District

Developmental stage reported by classroom teacher after a spelling inventory was conducted	Number of Students	SAT-9 % Range	Average SAT-9 %
Letter Name	4	1–15	8
Within-Word Pattern	30	4–68	32
Syllables and Affixes	38	15–99	62
Derivational Relations	18	49–99	90

Figure 2–2. SAT-9 and Developmental Stage Correlation (Los Peñasquitos Elementary School, Fourth and Fifth Graders, 1999–2000)

A printout of the spelling scores my class received on a norm-referenced test gives me limited information about my students' knowledge about spelling. All I know is that they are generally strong or weak in their knowledge of words; I have no idea why they are in the eighth rather than the eightieth percentile. On the other hand, if I take an inventory of their word knowledge by analyzing spelling errors to determine their stages of development, then I know what I have to teach. I now know what it takes to move a child from the letter name stage to the within-word pattern stage, which just may also move her or him from the eighth to the eightieth percentile on the standardized test. I would much rather design my instruction around a performance assessment that I can give any time I need to than wait until the June test results are in to find out if my teaching was effective.

It's All About Assessment

To understand spelling development means we must (a) know about the nature of the spelling system—the different layers of information the system reflects, and (b) know what students understand about these layers of information at different points along a developmental continuum.

—*Shane Templeton and Donald Bear*

Teachers should be aware of the stages of development and of the characteristics of each stage so that they can analyze the different strategies that children use when writing unknown words. Through this awareness, teachers will have an increased understanding of the logic behind children's spelling and should consequently be aware that errors may be due to the child's development and limited exposure to words, rather than an inability to spell.

—*Faye Bolton and Diane Snowball*

James Gleick recently wrote a book called *Faster: The Acceleration of Just About Everything* (2000) in which he describes the developmental nature of biological systems and our societal need for speed. In it, he tells a funny story about a woman who asked him how she could make the compost material in her backyard decompose at a faster rate. The absurdity of her question made him laugh out loud. He politely explained to the woman that it's a natural biological process that just takes time; we can't make it go any faster.

At around the same time as I was reading Gleick's book, I saw a cartoon in the Sunday paper. The first frame showed two men looking at a seemingly dead plant. They were just staring at it. In the second frame, one of the men screamed, "DO SOMETHING!" In the final frame, the plant miraculously bloomed. The other man looked shocked and then suggested that his friend might want to consider becoming a botanist.

I have also saved a cartoon in which a child boasts to a friend that he has just taught his dog how to whistle. His friend protests that he doesn't hear the dog whistling. The child then proudly responds, "I said I *taught* him how to whistle; I didn't say he *learned* it."

Each of these humorous examples is a metaphor for what can go wrong when spelling instruction consists of nothing but assignments. As we have seen, traditional approaches to spelling instruction focus on *assigning* and *correcting* rather than on *teaching* and *learning*. Assignments are handed out, worksheets are completed, and weekly spelling tests are memorized. This cycle repeats itself, week after week, with little or no regard for what a child is ready to learn or what a child has already learned. As many teachers have learned the hard way, just teaching the linguistic features or assigning lists to memorize will not guarantee that a child will learn the words. How many times have we dutifully completed week after week of spelling lists and workbook assignments wondering if it's doing any good? Even if the words you assign *are* developmentally appropriate for your students, rote assignments without active inquiry and engagement will not produce the lasting results you want.

What About Spelling Tests/Lists?

Have you ever heard a teacher say (or even said yourself), "I'm done teaching spelling this year because I finished the workbook"? Are we really *teaching* spelling when we give a pretest on Monday, provide homework activities during the week, and give a final test on Friday? Or are we merely assigning and testing spelling? How is a teacher to make sense of the best approach when conflicting theories abound?

You know what teachers admit quietly to one another when parents are not around: "I know spelling tests are not enough. They do not work. But I have to give them because the parents expect it!" This sort of professional trickery only adds to the mythology that weekly tests are appropriate as the organizing structure and central method for spelling instruction. If good spelling is based solely on memorization, then weekly tests should do the trick; but we know that excellent spellers rely on more than one strategy. Clearly, memorization is important, but it is not the only tool we need to teach students.

If teachers know that weekly spelling tests do not work, why are we still giving them? Simply put, the tests are expected by parents and easy to give. We can track, record, reward, and expect some students to score well on a weekly spelling test, with very little work on our part. Since many students live up to these expectations by consistently earning high spelling grades, no one (ourselves included) has any reason to question our practices. Tests seem to be working, and parents are happy because they have hard data, in the form of weekly spelling grades, that their child is succeeding or needs help. The status quo works perfectly well until we ask more questions. What does that weekly grade mean? Why do we give weekly tests? How do we choose the words for the tests? What are the students developmentally ready to learn? These questions make it almost impossible to ignore the fact that a student's ability to spell well in daily writing experiences has little to do with weekly spelling tests.

A question I'm often asked is whether copying words over and over is helpful for spelling. Schlagal (1998) puts this tired practice to rest in the following synthesis of research on the topic:

> The antiquated practice of writing words repeatedly until they were committed to memory gave way to the practice method wherein

missed words were rewritten correctly three times. Respecting this more modest practice, Henderson states that the aspirin principle should apply: "One helps a lot; two are almost twice as helpful, a third adds very little more, and four are bad for the stomach." In fact, copying a word over correctly more than three times appears to be counterproductive, affecting the quality of attention and inducing students to apply desperate measures like writing all the first letters first, then all the second letters, and so on, destroying the kinesthetic image which is a legitimate part of word knowledge.

Finally, a clear, concise way to explain to parents why copying words ten times isn't helpful!

The Word-Crafting Alternative

If you think about gardening, you will discover some similarities to word crafting. You would never, for example, plant a cactus next to a pond or try to grow a fern in a desert. The same is true for students studying phonics and spelling. They are ready for different things at different points in their development. It's our job to figure out what they are ready to explore. Figuring this out is where the static system of linguistic knowledge blends with the dynamic system of human development and learning. Ask a linguist *what* a child needs to learn about spelling, but when it comes to *when* the child should be learning to spell, ask an educator who understands developmental stages of learning. Educators who are knowledgeable about the developmental nature of teaching and learning are better able to suggest an appropriate sequence. A well-designed spelling inventory (see pp. 39–41) blends the knowledge of linguistics with the developmental stages of learning.

Spelling Inventories

When I began using a formal "spelling inventory" as an assessment tool, I soon realized how much I had been missing by virtually ignoring my students' developing knowledge of words. I now know that weekly spelling tests do not count as assessments *for* learning. They do not inform our instruction or lead to insights about spelling stages. At best, they are assessments *of* learning; all they show us is whether or not a child has memorized a list of words. A spelling inventory, on the other hand, is designed to be an assessment *for* learning because it provides information about the learner and guides instructional decisions and insight into what our students know.

There are many different inventories available for classroom use, but my favorites are the ones contained in *Words Their Way* (Bear et al. 1995, 1999, 2003) and *Word Journeys* (Ganske 2000). They all accomplish the goal of pinpointing the stage a student has reached. The inventories in *Words Their Way* were developed based on one published by Donald Bear and Diane Barone in an article titled "Using Children's Spellings to Group for Word Study and Directed Reading in the Primary Classroom" (1989). The authors introduce the concept of using an inventory along with an important message to anyone seeking to use them:

> It is important to remember that the results of this testing will not inform the teacher as to the specific orthographic patterns the student has or has not mastered. During this initial assessment, what the teacher should try to do is *estimate* the stage of development for each child by observing patterns in the child's correct and incorrect spellings. A gestalt of the child's spelling development and level of orthographic awareness should be the result.

In other words, the goal of the inventory is to get an overall sense of word knowledge and stage.

I've now been using spelling inventories for six years. At first, I found them very difficult and time-consuming, but I am now able to determine a child's spelling stage even without using a formal inventory. Using inventories over and over has taught me how to recognize the developmental spelling stages in students' writing. Perhaps the most important use of an inventory is that it provides a new set of lenses to help teachers look at spelling qualitatively. Using the inventory, I learned how to analyze spelling miscues, and my knowledge has now generalized so that I'm able to evaluate *any* misspelled word. The time invested in grading inventories was well spent.

The early versions of the inventories from *Words Their Way* were cumbersome, so I revised them to make them more "teacher-friendly" for my district to use. Early mistakes in using a spelling inventory may lead teachers down a misguided path of thinking that if a student misses the short *a* sound (for example), she or he has to engage in word study about short *a*. The knowledge we gain from a spelling inventory is *not* a list of three or four linguistic features for students to learn. Remember that at each stage there are many features to be explored, not just the few that appear on the inventory.

The inventories in *Word Journeys* explicitly break down each spelling stage and provide a separate inventory for each stage. I remember Donald Bear once saying, "It's not about teaching short *a* or long *e,* it's more about 'short vowelness' and 'long vowelness.'" Don't assume that just because a student gets a particular feature right on an inventory that the child has "learned" or "mastered" that feature. The inventory is designed to tell us the stage at which the student's linguistic knowledge begins to break down. When a student is clearly beyond the letter name stage, for example, misspelled words are *rarely* due to missing a short vowel, a blend, or a digraph because the student is no longer *confusing* those aspects of written language. While at that stage, though, a student may get short *a* right on some words on some days and miss the same feature the next day on a different word. This is what Bear et al. refer to as "using, but confusing" (1999, 15). The work is related to the bigger stage picture, not the individual features.

The biggest question teachers have once they correctly determine a spelling stage is, "What do I teach students at this stage?" Figure 3–1 shows the stages and the features to be learned at each stage of development.

Understanding How Students Think at the Letter Name Stage

Short vowel *sounds* are used but often confused with the *name* of the letter. Words with the short *a* sound are usually spelled correctly, because the short *a* sound is very similar to the *name* of the letter *A*. Other short vowel sounds are often misrepresented because they are based on the sounds the names of the letters make (but those letter name sounds are not the same as the vowel sound).

For example, a student at the letter name stage is quite likely to spell the word *pet* with the letter *a*: *pat*. Here's why: make the short *e* sound with your mouth, "eh, eh, eh." Now try to match the sound you are making with the name of one of the vowels. Does the "eh, eh, eh" sound match the letter name *E*? Not really. Feel the shape your mouth makes when you say "eh, eh, eh" compared to when you say "eeee." "Eh, eh, eh" sounds more like the letter name *A* more than it matches the letter name *E*. The shape of your mouth when you say "ay" is very close to the shape of your mouth when you say "eh." That's why letter name spellers substitute the long vowel *a* for the short *e* sound. They are almost "feeling" the sounds based on the shape of their mouth. For a much more detailed explanation of this concept, see Louisa Moats' book *Spelling Development, Disability, and Instruction* (1995, 37).

Prephonemic—Emergent Stage Ages: 1–7 Grades: Prekindergarten–Early First	
Characteristics:	**Linguistic Features to Be Learned:**
• Knows the names of some letters. • Can write some letters. • Scribbles. • Makes drawings. • No sound-symbol relationship. • Writing may be from left to right, up and down, or even backward. • Often pairs a random mix of letters with a picture.	Concept of a *word* How to notice symbols
Letter Name—Alphabetic Stage Ages: 5–7 Grades: Kindergarten–Early Third	
Characteristics:	**Linguistic Features to Be Learned:**
• Knows the names of each letter. • Experiments with sounds of letters. • Usually writes words with one or two letters, often the first or last letter heard in the word. • Generally leaves out vowels; spells words with consonants only. • Some words reflect correct use of short vowels (see short-vowel discussion below). • Not all sounds in the word are represented in child's approximation. (For example, Glenda Bissex [1980] reported these spellings from her five-year-old son: RUDF [*Are you deaf?*] and HAPE-BRTDA [*Happy Birthday*].) • Sounds that adults no longer hear are represented, because children spell speech sounds they actually hear. For *tree*, a student will often write *chree*; for *drink*, a child will often write *jrink*. They hear the *ch* sound for *tr* or the *j* sound for *dr*. • Two-letter units (digraphs like *ch* and *sh*) are learned early.	<u>Initial consonants</u> *b, m, r, s* *p, n, t, g* *c, f, d, g* *j, k, l, w* <u>Final consonants</u> *d, t, s, ll, g, f* <u>Short *a*, CVC word family</u> *ad, an, at, ag, ap, ar, all, ack, ang* <u>Short *e*, CVC word family</u> *ed, et, en, eg, ell, eck* <u>Short *i*, CVC word family</u> *it, ig, id, in, ip, ill, ick, ing, ink, ir* <u>Short *o*, CVC word family</u> *ot, ob, og, op, ock, ox* <u>Short *u* CVC word family</u> *ut, ub, ug, um, un, up, uff, ush, ump, ur* <u>Digraphs</u> *ch, sh, th, wh*

Figure 3–1. Developmental Spelling Sequence

	Linguistic Features to Be Learned:
	<u>s blends</u> *sp, sn, sm, st, sk, sw* <u>r blends</u> *br, cr, dr, fr, gr, pr, tr, wr* <u>l blends</u> *bl, cl, fl, gl, pl, sl* <u>More blends</u> *ck, nd, ng, nk* <u>Easy contractions and beginning homophones</u> *sp, sn, sm, st, sk, sw* <u>Final sound /y/ as in *puppy* and *lady*</u> <u>Adding *s* to naming words</u>

Within-Word Pattern Stage **Ages: 6–9** **Grades: 1–4**	
Characteristics:	**Linguistic Features to Be Learned:**
• Students recognize and use patterns and word families. • Beginning and ending consonants are consistently correct. • Short vowels are nearly always correct. • Long vowels are being explored as generalizations begin to govern spelling patterns. • Overgeneralizations of spelling patterns (silent *e* markers added to any word with a long vowel) may occur. • Most high frequency words are spelled correctly.	<u>Long *a*</u> *a_e* (*cave*), *ai* (*rain*), *ay* (*play*) Less common: *ei* (*eight*), *ey* (*prey*), *ea* (*great*) <u>Long *e*</u> *ee* (*green*), *ea* (*team*), *_e* (*me*), *e_e* (*theme*) Less common: *ie* (*chief*), *y* or *ey* (*lazy, key*) <u>Long *i*</u> *i_e* (*tribe*), *igh* (*sight*), *_y* (*fly*) Less common: *i* followed by *nd* or *ld* (*mind* or *child*) <u>Long *o*</u> *o_e* (*home*), *oa* (*float*), *ow* (*grow*) Less common: *o* followed by two consonants (*cold, most, jolt*) <u>Long *u*</u> *u_e* (*flute*), *oo* (*moon*), *ew* (*blew*) Less common: *ue* (*blue*), *ui* (*suit*)

Figure 3–1. *Continued*

	Linguistic Features to Be Learned:
	<u>r-controlled vowels</u> *a* with *r*: *ar* (*car*), *are* (*care*), *air* (*fair*) *e* with *r*: *er* (*her*), *eer* (*deer*), *ear* (*dear*) *i* with *r*: *ir* (*shirt*), *ire* (*fire*) *o* with *r*: *or* (*for*), *ore* (*store*), *our* (*pour*) *u* with *r*: *ur* (*burn*), *ure* (*cure*)
	<u>Diphthongs and vowel digraphs</u> *oy*, as in *boy* *oi*, as in *boil* *ou*, as in *cloud* *ow*, as in *brown* *ô*, as in *jaw* *oo*, as in *moon* *oo*, as in *book*
	<u>Middle-level homophones and middle-level contractions</u> *ough* and *augh*
	<u>/j/ sound, as in *dodge, giraffe, jump*</u> <u>/s/ sound, as in *city, place, circus*</u>

Syllables and Affixes Stage
Ages: 8–18
Grades: 3–8

Characteristics:	**Linguistic Features to Be Learned:**
• Initial blends and digraphs are always correct. • Short vowels are always correct. • Long vowel patterns are almost always correct. • All sounds in each syllable are represented, although not always correctly. • Silent letters are beginning to be used correctly. • Consonant doubling is not always correct.	<u>Single-syllable homophones</u> *bear/bare/Bayer* *meet/meat* *rode/road* *sea/see* <u>Plural endings</u> Add *s* and add *es* Change *y* to *i* <u>Compound words</u> 2-syllable: *aircraft, airplane* 3-syllable: *anywhere, however* <u>Simple inflectional endings</u> VCC–_*ask*: *asked, asking* VVC–_*aim*: *aimed, aiming*

Figure 3–1. *Continued*

	Linguistic Features to Be Learned:
	Consonant doubling *bat: batting, batted*
	Stress and accent Open and closed syllables: VCCV, VCV, VCCCV, and VV patterns
	Prefixes and suffixes
	Silent consonants *knee, write*
	Other ways to spell /sh/ *polish, motion, electrician, mission*
	Spelling *ie* or *ei* *thief, piece, neighbor*

Derivational Patterns Stage **Ages: 10–Adult** **Grades: 5–12**	
Characteristics:	**Linguistic Features to Be Learned:**
• Most words are spelled conventionally. • All blends, digraphs, short vowels, long vowels, other vowel patterns, double consonants, prefixes, and suffixes are spelled correctly. • Misspellings indicate an error in morphology and etymology.	Consonant changes Silent to sounded (*soften* to *soft*) /t/ to /sh/ (*select* to *selection*) /k/ to /sh/ (*music* to *musician*) Vowel changes long to short (*crime* to *criminal*) long to schwa (*define* to *definition*) short to schwa (*legality* to *legal*) Greek and Latin word elements Origins of words words from Spanish and French words from places words new to English Unusual plurals Words often confused or mispronounced

Sources: Henderson (1990); Templeton (1986); Bissex (1980); and Moats (1995)

Figure 3–1. *Continued*

Another interesting characteristic of students at the letter name stage of spelling development is that they have a solid understanding of the *name* of each letter in the alphabet but their understanding of the *sounds* of these letters is not secure. Therefore, their spelling approximations are informed largely by their solid knowledge of letter names. This knowledge of sounds is what they are using but still confusing. It is, however, important to understand that even within this "using but confusing" application of spelling knowledge there are very predictable patterns of students' encoding miscues. Thanks to the groundbreaking work of Charles Read (1971), we know that the error patterns children make as they learn to spell are predictable and regular, and they follow a clear developmental continuum. Students at this stage often use the name of the letter in order to guess the sound of the letter. This strategy only works some of the time. Problems occur when the *name* of the letter has nothing to do with the *sound* of the letter; think, for example, of the letter *W.* The name of the letter, "double u," is nothing like the sound of the letter, "wuh."

Figure 3–2 summarizes the typical encoding errors that letter name spellers might make as they approximate standard spelling. Since students at this stage are spelling by sound, not by pattern or meaning (which are later stages), the sound is listed first (in the left-hand columns) and then the letter the student might use to represent that sound is listed in the next column.

I find Vygotsky's (1978) description of the learner's "zone of proximal development"—the cognitive space in which a learner has the greatest potential for new learning—helpful when I am trying to decide how much assistance to give a student. This zone is the difference between what the child can do without any assistance and what a child can only do with help. The easiest way to understand this concept is to think about it as the Goldilocks theory: you want to make your teaching not "too hard," not "too soft [easy]," but "just right." In order to determine

Sound the Student Hears	Letter the Student Might Use for That Sound
e, a	a
b	b
s	c
d	d
i, e	e
ef	f
j, ch	g
ch, sh	h
tr	hr
o, i	i
j, ch	j
dr	jr
c, k	k
el	l
m	m
n	n
u, o	o
p	p
k	q
or	r
s, sh	s
t, th	t
oo, u	u
v, th	v
d	w
ex	x
w	y
z	z

Figure 3–2. Sound/Symbol Associations Made by Letter Name Spellers

what is "just right" for the learner, you need to examine what the student appears to be doing with extreme ease and "automaticity." You also need to watch for that moment when the learner begins to experience frustration and exhibits a lack of spelling sophistication. And finally, you need to pay the most attention when the learner is beginning to understand a concept, and may at times seem to grasp it, but at other times gets it wrong.

Knowledgeable Teachers Move Beyond the Inventories

Before I learned about these stages of spelling development, I used to look at spelling only quantitatively: either a word was spelled correctly or it was spelled incorrectly. By studying developmental spelling theory, using inventories of word knowledge, and analyzing student spelling, I have learned to look at student spelling qualitatively as well: the *way* the word is misspelled tells me what the child is ready to learn. As I said, I don't even have to use an inventory anymore to understand what the child knows about our spelling system. I've learned to recognize what a child is doing by framing a few questions as I look over the work.

Three important questions to ask yourself when you are analyzing student spelling are:

1. Which features is the student using correctly?

2. Which features is the student using but confusing?

3. Which features are missing in the student's knowledge of spelling?

After you use these techniques and ideas for a while, you will find (as I did) that they become automatic; you will apply these questions to evaluate student spelling without having to refer to any inventory or text.

Grades are not determined by these questions, but instruction becomes more focused because we are able to zoom in on a child's developmental stage and teach what the child is ready to learn. Our own knowledge of the features needs to be solid to help us analyze the errors we see. It might take some practice and some learning on your part to understand the most typical linguistic features that students at your grade level are ready to explore. The more you know about these, the better you are able to explore with your students what they need to learn.

Cheryl Ritter, an excellent teacher who works in the San Diego area, has worked hard to create a word-crafting classroom. She understands the importance of being informed by the patterns she observes in her students' work. After attending one of my workshops, she wrote me the following letter:

> Dear Cindy,
>
> It was great to see you again today, and to hear your spelling presentation. A lot of things "clicked" for me. The various levels of the spelling inventories will be helpful, and I especially like the classroom composites [see Appendix J]. I also like the way you tied in the SAT-9 assessments with the levels. I think it's helpful to see that there is a correlation.
>
> I worked up that spelling analysis sheet I showed you using the developmental stages. I geared it to the intermediate grades, and then I tried out all my students on it, since I already had lists of misspelled words I'd found in their writing. Sure enough, I was able to really *see* where their problems were, and where they were developmentally at the same time.
>
> I'm excited about all of this. If you have time, please give me feedback on the form. I'd be happy to keep working on it and I'd like to pass it on to any teachers at my school who might want to try it too.
>
> Take care,
> Cheryl

Cheryl has taken the power of what she learned using inventories with preselected words and applied it to students' words from their real writing (see her analysis sheet in Figure 3–3). It's an easy task to collect ten or so misspelled words from your student's writing and do your own qualitative analysis of the errors you see. Are most of the errors related to letter name—is the student missing initial/final consonants, short vowels, blends, and digraphs? Or do the errors have more to do with within-word pattern—is the student getting all the initial/final consonants, short vowels, blends, and digraphs correct but missing long vowel and other vowel patterns? There is not an exact science to this, but you are looking for patterns of understanding and misunderstanding.

Ultimately, I believe that the significance of this work is being able to conduct a spelling inventory "on the run" like a running record. We should be able to look at any piece of writing and quickly determine the student's spelling stage. I appreciate Richard Gentry's (2000) take on the orthodoxy about spelling stages that seems to be forming. His article carefully points out that stage theories based solely on linguistic elements are missing the other aspects of language development. He prefers to take a more global approach to stages and incorporates qualitative differences in how the student *thinks* at each stage instead of just looking at the linguist patterns that he argues "may be better characterized as descriptions of invented spellings within stages, not spelling stages themselves."

Gentry also wrote an excellent *Reading Teacher* article (1982) in which he analyzes the developmental spelling found in Glenda Bissex's book *GNYS at Work*. He helps shed light on the developmental nature of learning to spell by describing the stages that Paul (Bissex's son) went through as he learned to spell. His analysis focuses on the child, not on the tiny, minute linguistic features to be learned at each stage. It's a far more global approach and reminds me of what Donald Graves does in his book *Writing: Teachers and Children at Work*. He looks at what the children are actually doing as they learn to write. From there, the now common "writing process" emerges as almost

Spelling Analysis

Student _____ Date _____ Page _____

Word	STAGES				Letter Name			Within Word			Syllables and Affixes			Derivational Relations	
	Student Spelling	Spelling Demon	Homo-phone	Short Vowels	Digraphs (i.e., sh, ch, wh, th, ck)	Blends (i.e., nk, sl, st, dr, tr)	Long Vowels	Vowel Teams/ Dipthong and R-controlled Vowels	Complex Cons.	Syllable Juncture/ Cons. Doubling	Prefixes	Suffixes and Endings	Vowels in the Middle	Bases and Roots

Figure 3–3. Spelling Analysis Form

sacrosanct steps (prewriting, writing, sharing, revising, editing). If Graves had simply told us the steps of writing, the writing workshop would be empty. Instead he focuses on what the child does inside these steps and shows us how to attend to the child's behavior. In the same way the linguistic features in spelling are just the observable artifacts of a complex stage that can't be reduced to "learn the long *e* sound."

Here are Gentry's stages:

1. *The pre-communicative stage.* The child thinks spelling is putting letters together but does not think about matching specific letters to sounds.

2. *The semiphonetic stage.* The child recognizes that letters may correspond to sounds, but generally is unable to segment all the sounds in the word or match the letters to all the sounds. The spelling of a word is abbreviated or it may contain extra letters that don't match sounds in the word. All semiphonetic spellings do have some letters that match some of the sounds in the word.

3. *The phonetic stage.* The child uses a sound-based strategy as the dominant strategy. He or she thinks the way to invent a spelling is to listen to the sounds and then match a letter to each sound. Full phonemic awareness is usually evident; that is, the child can now segment the speech sounds in most words he or she tries to spell. Additionally, all the sounds in the word are represent in the spelling. (One exception is the spelling of preconsonantal nasals where the *M* or *N* in words like *STAP* [stamp] or *STAD* [stand] are systematically omitted.)

4. *The transitional stage.* The child uses a visual and morphologically based strategy as the dominant strategy. He or she no longer invents spellings by thinking only about the sound in the word, but uses letters, patterns, or letter sequences he or she remembers seeing in print to spell corresponding sounds. Visual conventions such as

vowel in every syllable, *e* marker patterns, vowel digraphs, and common English letter sequences remembered from other spellings are used.

5. *The correct stage (conventional stage).* Each year beyond the transitional stage the child adds to the store of words he or she can spell correctly and extends his or her knowledge about words and patterns.

By blending what I learned from Gentry's stages, which show how the child thinks (along with the features that are part of the growing system in the child's repertoire) with the stages presented in *Words Their Way*, I have developed deeper, more informed knowledge about my students' spelling development. It was an important insight to realize that the features are less important than the "homogeneity" of how the child thinks at each stage.

When I realized that "the child thinks basically the same way whenever he or she invents a spelling at a particular stage," I gained a greater insight into evaluating student spelling than I would ever see in an inventory that directed me only to the phonics and linguistics on the page. Gentry says it quite well: "She or he may list random letters (pre-communicative), or use a sound-based strategy as the dominant strategy (phonetic spelling, by ear), or use a visually based strategy as the dominant strategy (transitional spelling, by eye)."

If you read *Words Their Way*, instead of just looking at or using the inventory (which is what most people do), you can see that the same theoretical underpinnings led to the development of the inventories. The inventories are just a way to focus our attention on features. We need to know the thinking behind the features we see and we need to be able to apply what we know when we look at any piece of student writing, not just a spelling inventory.

After reading an article by Mary Jo Fresch (2001), I designed an activity to help teachers learn how to determine spelling stages by looking at journal samples. I went through several months of journal entries in various classrooms, choosing one or two students at each grade level. Then I wrote down ten words that I found misspelled in each of their journals and gave the lists to teachers to analyze (see Figure 3–4). They looked for the reason each word was misspelled and were able to determine a spelling stage based on the type of error. They circled the predicted stage in the list I had provided on the bottom of the page. (This demonstration won't work as well with teachers who have not spent time using an inventory. It's a better tool to use to show teachers how to apply what they've learned by doing inventories to looking at spelling in context.)

It is very easy to underestimate the importance of assessment. One of my favorite lines is from a very thoughtful teacher at my school who felt overwhelmed and frustrated by all of the assessments we had to do. She would often say that she just wanted to get "back to teaching the kids." One day at lunch, she stormed into the staff room in a huff and exclaimed, "When are we going to stop weighing the cows around here and start feeding them?" It was an honest expression of frustration based on her perception that the tests were not helping her teach. After that, though, I started wondering whether having to give so many assessments was really the problem. After thinking long and hard about her comment, I came to the conclusion that maybe it wasn't that we were assessing too much—it was that we didn't know how to use the assessments to drive our instruction. *Assessment drives instruction* is our district's mantra. We firmly believe, from the leadership in our district office right down to the principals and the teachers, that any assessment tool we use has to be meaningful and inform our instruction. It has to help us to decide the next best step for instruction.

All too often our instruction is focused on what we, as teachers, need to teach the child. Why not find out what the child is ready to

Child A		Child B		Child C	
1. bk	(back)	1. hert	(hurt)	1. fihgthers	(fighters)
2. frum	(from)	2. scaree	(scary)	2. picher	(picture)
3. hr	(her)	3. inof	(enough)	3. reson	(reason)
4. lik	(like)	4. rochereyer	(retriever)	4. larn	(learn)
5. los	(loose)	5. youers	(years)	5. grate	(great)
6. toof	(tooth)	6. drass	(dress)	6. firy	(furry)
7. fis	(friends)	7. prtand	(pretend)	7. peoplole	(people)
8. kitin	(kitten)	8. fourst	(first)	8. yous	(use)
9. seryol	(cereal)	9. weale	(wheel)	9. yumey	(yummy)
10. tac	(take)	10. chert	(shirt)	10. thout	(thought)

Child D		Child E		Child F	
1. commplete	(complete)	1. lier	(liar)	1. inbarise	(embarrass)
2. easely	(easily)	2. scater	(scatter)	2. devous	(devious)
3. anoyed	(annoyed)	3. goble	(gobble)	3. mischevious	(mischievous)
4. wold	(would)	4. controll	(control)	4. certinly	(certainly)
5. choped	(chopped)	5. trespase	(trespass)	5. supirior	(superior)
6. devilesh	(devilish)	6. proprty	(property)	6. gullabole	(gullible)
7. quils	(quills)	7. likeable	(likable)	7. teradactol	(pterodactyl)
8. qweshin	(question)	8. practiacly	(practically)	8. amazzing	(amazing)
9. witch	(which)	9. write	(right)	9. prezident	(president)
10. fowl	(foul)	10. tryes	(tries)	10. goverment	(government)

Are the errors due to: • Initial/final consonants • Short vowels • Blends or digraphs If so, the student is probably a Letter Name speller.	*Are the errors due to:* • Consonant doubling • Prefixes or suffixes • Dropping or changing letters when suffix is added If so, the student is probably a Syllables and Affixes speller.
Are the errors due to: • Long vowels • Other vowel patterns If so, the student is probably a Within Word Pattern speller.	*Are the errors due to:* • Latin or Greek roots • Knowledge of word derivation If so, the student is probably a Derivational Relations speller.

Figure 3–4. Analyzing Spelling in Student Writing

learn? The way I see it, if we want to design instructional opportunities for them to practice what they are developmentally ready to learn, timing is essential. Timing becomes far more important than content; and assessment is critical.

Determining Groups in Your Class Based on Assessment

While some may say that it's just too difficult to manage multiple groups for instruction, others see the vast potential and huge educational returns that result when you carefully form groups based on students' instructional needs. To me, it just doesn't make sense not to place students purposefully in instructional groups based on similar needs.

I would certainly never recommend putting a child into a group for an entire year based on only one test result. Once teachers have assigned students to groups by relying on multiple measures and drawing on their professional judgment, I find that purposeful grouping actually honors children more than heterogeneous grouping does. We need to commit ourselves to assessing our students, and then let the assessment inform our grouping decisions and instruction. Our students will thrive when they are placed in learning situations in which they are able to extend what they currently know. This is the critical zone of proximal development that Vygotsky outlined in his 1978 research. Students learn best when they are encouraged to reach just beyond their current ability. How can we create a "ripe for learning" zone for each student? The key is continuous reassessment, moving students in and out of groups as needed.

Analyzing Spelling Errors

The power of word-crafting spelling instruction can be illustrated in this simple story. Not long ago I was working with a third grader whose teacher was concerned about his progress. She saw him as a "struggling student," and she called an SAT (Student Assistance Team) meeting with the parents to determine what was causing delays in his development. Her chief concern was his spelling. I asked his teacher to give me several of his writing samples (his class work spanned September through January), and I also gave him the Elementary Qualitative Spelling Inventory (Bear et al. 1999, 288). When I began analyzing his journal entries, an intriguing pattern surfaced. Here is what I found:

- Almost all the high frequency words were spelled correctly.
- His misspelled words were at an appropriate stage for a third grader.
- However, many of his errors didn't make sense to me, so I made the following list of spelling errors I found in his writing:

Correct Spelling	*David's Spelling*
float	flont
beaches	benches
would	wond
forget	frgent
had	hand
water	wanter
watching	wonching
that	tant
watch	wonch
lot	lonch

Do you see the pattern? I was very curious about what at first seemed to be random placements of the letter *n*. Then I noticed that he inserted the letter *n* before the consonants *t* and *d* and the blends *ch* or *tch*. Each time there was an *n*, it was before the letter *t* or *d* or the blend *ch* or *tch*. This didn't seem to fit with any of the typical errors I had learned to look for. For example, I am not usually concerned about an average third grader spelling the word *float* as *flot* at the beginning of the year, but *flont* was odd. So, I decided to test out my theory. I developed a test just for David so that I would have a chance to see if he was overgeneralizing the use of the letter *n* to other consonant sounds. (I wasn't concerned that the test was not authentic writing, because I had already collected samples of his authentic writing; I was merely testing my hypothesis.)

Here is the test I gave him, along with the spellings he generated:

Correct Spelling	David's Spelling
cold	colnd (I knew I was on to something right away!)
reach	rench
boat	bont
caught	cont
wet	went
catch	canch
hot	hont
chat	chant
mad	mand
each	ench
about	abont
could	cound
had	hand

Now I knew! It was so exciting to see where David was "using but confusing" a generalization that he had made up. It was incorrect, but it was consistent. I could see that reteaching and specific intervention would be necessary.

The critical piece of this story is that, after giving the second assessment, I needed to ask David what he was thinking as he spelled those words. I asked him, "Tell me about how you spelled *wet*." He showed me how he sounded it out by saying the sounds for *w* and then *e* and then he enunciated the sound for *t* correctly, but he wrote *nt*. I asked him how he knew to put *nt* for the *t* sound. He then showed me what his mouth does when he says *nt*. His tongue touches the roof of his mouth just like it does when you make the *n* sound. Try it. Make the *t* sound and now make the *n* sound. Feel where your tongue is. It's the same tongue placement for both letters. During further inquiry and discussion he told me that the letter *d* does the same thing. So, when his tongue touches the roof of his mouth as in *t, ch,* and *d,* it is the same motion as in the *n* sound, which is why he writes the *n*.

This was fascinating, and most important, his face absolutely lit up when he saw that I understood what he was doing. I've since developed some word study activities to do with him. We spend time doing word games and word sorts with rimes, using the *ad, ed, id, od* rimes and the *at, et, it, ot, ut* rimes (and the same with *ch* and *tch*).

It is my sincere hope that every single one of you has the opportunity to apply your knowledge in this manner—to happen on something in a child's learning life that causes all your theories and knowledge to crystallize. That's what it was like for me as I worked with David. I thought I had already learned a lot about developmental spelling theory; but until I encountered David's thinking, what I knew was just surface knowledge, theory, pedagogy.

This was just the beginning for me. After you have had experiences like this, you will wonder how you ever taught spelling without knowing how to look closely and to recognize what you are seeing. It's like getting a pair of prescription glasses after needing them for years. When my husband finally gave in and put on a pair of glasses for the first time, he commented, "Before I had glasses, all street signs were good for was to tell me what street I had just passed; I needed to have that information while I still had time to do something with it." That also rings true for me and my experiences with spelling analysis.

Essential Classroom Practices

Teaching is not telling. Teachers cannot teach students how to spell by telling them the rules, no matter how explicit ... that require kids to do so.

—*The Elementary School Journal*

The developmental position crucially impacts the teacher's role. No longer a passive program manager, an effective spelling teacher must have an understanding of the nature of the English spelling system itself as well as knowledge of the stages through which children pass as they learn to spell. To improve spelling instruction, we need more informed teachers schooled in the demands of English spelling and familiar with what children must know to meet its demands.

—*Laurie Nelson*

You've done the assessments—now what? You're over the hurdle of learning how to use an inventory, and you face the next big challenge. You have much more precise information about what your students are capable of learning, now you need to create the atmosphere that will allow them to learn it. You need to increase children's spelling consciousness, teach them spelling strategies and patterns, have them memorize high frequency words, and invite caregivers to participate as well. This is where most teachers get frustrated.

Perhaps the most important shift in my thinking about how to approach the teaching of spelling occurred while I was working as a guest teacher with a group of third graders. At that time, I really preferred to teach spelling strategies in the context of writing. I liked using "minilessons," and I relied heavily on Sandra Wilde's book *You Kan Red This!* (1992) to help me figure out which lessons to teach. I also valued invented spelling because it was a tool that allowed my regular class of second graders to write expressively without getting hung up on how to spell. They were comfortable with using invented spelling and I was content to let them use it, but I started calling it "temporary spelling" or "phonetic spelling" to placate parents who were concerned that I wasn't teaching "phonics." In the end, although I believed that my students were learning to spell through their writing and my minilessons, I still believed that they were missing out on some essential elements.

After reading *Words Their Way* (Bear et al. 1995, 1999, 2003) and many related articles (the list in Appendix D will get you started), I realized that I could become more purposeful in my approach and still provide developmentally appropriate lessons. I could honor children's voices and choices in their writing while also teaching them about how words work. I decided to work out a study sequence. From my research, I learned that an appropriate place to begin with third graders is "long vowel word study." However, all that I knew to be true about teaching reading and writing stemmed from the overriding principle that language has to be made meaningful to students, and the "long *a* sound" just didn't seem like something I could make meaningful. I was still not convinced that teaching children about letter sounds was going to pave the road to excellent spelling. Even if average third graders were ready to learn long vowel patterns, they were still not relevant to their lives.

However, after spending ten weeks with that third-grade class exploring long vowels, focusing on the long vowel sounds at least as much as I did on creating opportunities for students to immerse themselves in reading and writing, my thinking shifted. We created a social context in which to explore the linguistic features of print as a group, to find out together how long vowels work. Each time I visited the class, the students responded with growing intrigue and enthusiasm; their level of engagement was heartening. By the third week, I began to be greeted with applause every time I arrived for our lesson. The children, even the most challenged spellers in the class, were truly excited by word study. Words came alive through the active participation of the group and the social nature of the learning, and I knew then how very important the social atmosphere is in a word-crafting classroom. (Word study notebooks associated with these lessons are included in Appendix E.)

The inventory hints at an underlying linguistic sequence. Features that students are typically using but confusing at each developmental stage are listed in Figure 3–1, in Chapter 3 (also see Appendix F for the spelling developmental phases in a nutshell). It's important to remember that just because a student gets the "long *a*" pattern correct on a test doesn't mean that she doesn't need more "long *a*" study. If you have appropriately identified her stage of spelling development, you will find that some days she will understand that feature and some days she won't. Remember that she's using—but confusing—the requisite linguistic features typical of that stage. For you as a teacher, it's not so much a matter of figuring out what features need to be learned but more a matter of understanding each stage and then immersing students in word study at that stage. Certainly, you will be teaching the features, but if you address the work one linguistic element at a time, you might not spend enough time exploring each feature. Also, the features do not need to be taught one at a time. I often teach several together as we work to find patterns, similarities, and differences.

Once a child has passed through a stage, she rarely misses the features that are most characteristic of that stage and will therefore no longer misspell those words. Solid word knowledge comes from immersion in word study that allows students to examine, inquire, and explore how words work. By attending to the features that correspond to the right developmental level, you will be able to provide this opportunity. You can gear your whole-class word study to the main stage represented by most of your students. Some teachers have several developmental spelling groups in their room. Some teachers team with a number of other teachers to divide the students by stage. Even if you address whole-class instruction to the dominant stage, your students who are above/below that stage will still benefit from the active engagement. You just need to be sure to address their needs, especially the lower levels, in their reading group or in some other manner.

The traditional approach to teaching spelling has every child in the class studying the same list of words. As you know, those traditional spelling lists vary greatly. Some are based on only one phonetic feature—*ee* words, for example. Some are based on more than one feature—long *a* and short *a*, for example (these are considered "pattern words"). Some teachers give weekly word lists that are grouped not by pattern but by frequency of use. Still other teachers make up personal lists of words individual students have misspelled in their writing.

I can't say it strongly enough: passing out word lists, giving tests, grading them, and then passing out a new list the next week is not teaching—it's assigning and correcting. It's administering memorization. Yet this is the norm, and parents and others assume that if so many teachers are approaching spelling this way, then it must be working: it must be the correct way.

With all we now know about the stages of development, it is professionally irresponsible to ignore them. As professionals, we have some decisions to make so that our approach to spelling instruction is meaningful. Initially, the word-crafting approach will involve more work on your part (taking inventories, figuring out the stages of development, and so on), but once you perfect it and see how easy it is to attain your goal of having children who can spell and are excited about language, you will find it far more rewarding and ultimately easier than traditional methods.

Essential Components for Word Study

"Is it okay to use a spelling workbook to teach spelling?" Well, that's like asking whether it's okay to use a hammer to build a table. The answer depends on how you plan to use it. Consider what you hope to accomplish with the workbook. It will serve you well first to decide on your goals before you decide what tools to use. Carve out a word-study program that allows for five basic components:

- Teaching students spelling strategies.
- Helping students memorize high frequency words.
- Teaching students to generalize spelling patterns.
- Creating conditions that develop students' spelling consciousness.
- Communicating with parents about your methods.

Of course your program must also include ongoing assessments, both formal and informal. Use inventories and real writing samples to continually monitor spelling knowledge and growth.

Teaching Students Spelling Strategies

> It is important for teachers to be aware of the strategies that competent spellers use in order to develop the use of such strategies by all children.
> —*Faye Bolton and Diane Snowball*

As adults, when we need to write a word that we don't know how to spell, we enter the same cognitive space that children occupy most of the time! Think about what you do when you don't know how to spell a word. I'm quite certain that you don't rely solely on the mantra so often repeated to children: *sound it out.* Too often, that is the only strategy we give our students. Of course, as adults, we still rely on the sound of the word when we need to. In fact, when we are challenged to spell a word that we have no knowledge of—for example, a foreign word like *Chapultepec*—we sometimes resort to the lowest level of word knowledge, sounding it out. If someone said the word *Chapultepec,* and asked me to spell it, I would first try to sound it out, but I would probably get stuck on the third vowel. Sound tells me it could be either an *e* or an *a.* I've never seen the word in print, so I couldn't write it down to see which version looked right. I could try to look it up in an encyclopedia or ask other people what they know about the word. My husband, for example, used to live near a park named *Chapultepec,* so if I happened to ask him, he would probably know, because he has seen it in print (on the park sign) many times. He has the advantage of being able to use visual memory cues (another kind of spelling strategy) to help him spell it, but I can only rely on sounding it out (or on my knowledge of word patterns and linguistic features).

Think about times when you are having trouble spelling a word. What strategies do you employ? Some of the strategies you might use are:

1. Your knowledge of the word history (morphology).

2. Your knowledge of the word's linguistic features.

3. Visual memory (such as a park sign).

4. Your ability to generalize the thousands of patterns you've internalized from your reading.

5. A memory device.

6. A dictionary.

7. Another person.

In a word-crafting classroom, it is sometimes interesting to compile a class-specific list of good spelling strategies with your students. Although the list may not be complete, the process helps the students feel engaged and to think about spelling strategies in an investigative way. Here is the list of strategies my group of third graders came up with:

- Look for patterns.
- Look for word parts.
- Try several ways to write a word.
- Write sounds in words.
- Write a vowel in each word and each syllable.
- Think about words that sound the same.
- Think about words that look the same.
- Check to see if words look right.
- Think about what a word means.
- Practice words.
- Use a dictionary to check spellings.
- Look for words in the classroom.
- Ask someone else for help.

Helping Students Memorize High Frequency Words

In 1990, my district decided to create its own spelling program rather than buy a published one. A team of teachers and reading specialists developed a comprehensive spelling curriculum based on Rebecca Sitton's Spelling Sourcebook program. Sitton gives talks at many state and national conferences and she presents a compelling argument that we should be teaching "high frequency" words, which make up 50 percent of all words used in writing. It just wouldn't make sense, according to Sitton, not to have our students learn these words by heart. Sitton's theory makes sense, but her influence led my district to create a core spelling curriculum based solely on the twelve hundred most frequently used words. As a consequence, we were only assigning spelling, rather than teaching it.

There is nothing wrong with asking students to memorize high frequency words, but this strategy alone isn't enough, especially in view of Cramer and Cipielewski's research (1995). They make a very important distinction between "high frequency" words and "frequently misspelled" words. Most of the word lists that we ask children to memorize are high frequency words (words that appear most often in print). The point Cramer and Cipielewski make is that it is fine to have students memorize some of these words, but many of them are not actually "problem" words for our students (for example, *a, the, to, for*).

This research team actually looked at thousands of samples of authentic writing and came up with the words that students most frequently misspell. They then compiled a list of the one hundred words that are most often misspelled, year in and year out (see Figure 4–1). They also developed lists of words that are most often misspelled at each grade level. I recommend taking a look at Ron Cramer's *The Spelling Connection* (1998) so that you too can rethink the words you are asking your students to memorize.

Teaching Students to Generalize Spelling Patterns

We also have to teach students to "generalize" spelling patterns and rules, because it is clearly impossible for anyone to memorize all the words that they will have to know. Knowing certain linguistic principles and patterns, and thus being able to predict how a word might be spelled, will improve children's ability to spell. When our word-study instruction includes helping our students discover and then generalize key spelling rules and patterns, the amount of correct spelling in student writing increases exponentially. We need to "scaffold" this learning to match our students' instructional and developmental levels. Some of the questions we need to consider are:

- Which patterns matter; which don't?
- When should I teach the patterns?
- Which patterns should I teach first?

1	too	26	didn't	51	like	76	about
2	a lot	27	people	52	whole	77	first
3	because	28	until	53	another	78	happened
4	there	29	with	54	believe	79	Mom
5	their	30	different	55	I'm	80	especially
6	that's	31	outside	56	thought	81	school
7	they	32	we're	57	let's	82	getting
8	it's	33	through	58	before	83	started
9	when	34	upon	59	beautiful	84	was
10	favorite	35	probably	60	everything	85	which
11	went	36	don't	61	very	86	stopped
12	Christmas	37	sometimes	62	into	87	two
13	were	38	off	63	caught	88	Dad
14	out	39	everybody	64	one	89	took
15	they're	40	heard	65	Easter	90	friend's
16	said	41	always	66	what	91	presents
17	know	42	I	67	there's	92	are
18	you're	43	something	68	little	93	morning
19	friend	44	would	69	doesn't	94	could
20	friends	45	want	70	usually	95	around
21	really	46	and	71	clothes	96	buy
22	finally	47	Halloween	72	scared	97	maybe
23	where	48	house	73	everyone	98	family
24	again	49	once	74	have	99	pretty
25	then	50	to	75	swimming	100	before

Figure 4–1. 100 Most Commonly Misspelled Words Across Eight Grade Levels (Cramer and Cipielewski 1995)

Here's an example of how this can work. One of my classes started an inquiry about when to use the word *a* and when to use *an*. Their word study research led them to the following generalizations:

- Use the article *a* before any word beginning with a consonant or long *u* vowel sound: *a* letter, *a* script, *a* unicorn.
- Use the article *an* before any vowel except the long *u* sound and before the silent *h*: *an* apricot, *an* honorarium, *an* increase.

Word sorts

In word-crafting classrooms, "word sorts" are centerpiece activities used to teach students to generalize the patterns and principles they are ready to explore. There are detailed descriptions about how to do word sorts in *Words Their Way*. Familiarize yourself with the various types of sorts and their purposes. A colleague of mine in San Diego has developed excellent resources for conducting sorts. Her books *All Sorts of Sorts* (Brown 2000, 2002, 2003) will give you the specifics you need about word sorts. You will also find help with sorting activities in many of the resources in Appendix D.

The anatomy of a spelling lesson

The energy and excitement in a well-planned word-study class is hard to miss. The students in the fifth-grade class I mentioned earlier frequently stopped me in the hall to talk about words. Words had become an important part of their lives, not just a school subject. They told me about going online at night to look up words and about using the dictionaries in their classroom to help them figure out words. One of their favorite games was one I modified from a spelling workbook. We called it the "spelling spree."

First, I assessed all of the students using multiple measures:

- I received the average spelling test scores from the teacher (who had implemented and finished the district spelling program by January and was concerned about what she was going to do for spelling for the rest of the year).
- I used the prebook test from a pilot copy of the Houghton Mifflin Spelling Series (almost every series has some sort of prebook test, a valuable tool if used with other measures).
- I determined their percentage score using the *Words Their Way* spelling inventory (Bear et al. 1995, 1999, 2003).
- Together, the teacher and I took their standardized test scores into consideration.
- I looked at samples of student writing from everyday assignments.

Then, with the results gathered from these assessment tools, the teacher and I grouped the class into three developmental stages.

On day 1, we set up our word-study notebooks. (I've included several for you to take a look at, in Appendix E.) By developing our own word-study notebooks, we were essentially writing our own spelling books for the year. Everything we did that was related to words went into these books. We set them up like real books. Students decorated the covers, wrote a dedication to someone who influenced their spelling, even made a table of contents.

On day 2, I gave students a word list of long *a* and long *e* words. They cut out the words and kept them in an envelope in their word-study notebooks. We then did an "open sort" in which they sorted the words any way that made sense to them. This was a new concept for them. In the beginning, the sorts were quite random. The categories they chose to sort told us a lot about their linguistic knowledge. The less sophisticated students tended to sort by categories like these:

- Things at home.
- Alphabetical order.
- Number of letters in the words.
- Alphabetical order by last letter (yes, I had a student try this one!).

On day 3, I stipulated the criteria for a closed sort. The students then sorted the words at their desks and recorded the sort into their word study notebooks. (Clearly long-vowel sounds are too simple for almost any fifth grader, but we started with them to give the class a sense of success.) Then I had them hunt for similar words in a recent read-aloud book.

On day 4, I introduced the "spelling spree." They absolutely loved this. Everyone began with the same word: *cat*. I then gave the class seven minutes to generate a list of words by only changing one letter at a time (proper nouns not allowed). For example:

cat
bat
mat
map
tap
tape
take
taker
maker
baker
biker
bicker

backer

hacker

etc.

Once seven minutes were up, each child came to the overhead projector and wrote down his or her words; the rest of us checked them for accuracy and assigned one point for each correct word. If one of the words on their list happened to be a long vowel word (the sound we were studying) the student received two points. The word-crafting environment was buzzing with conversation about the words.

By day 5 we had collected words with the long vowel sounds we were exploring and were able to make generalizations about the various ways long *a* and long *e* could be spelled. Try this with your students. See how many different ways the long *a* sound can be spelled. Here are some the ways we found to spell the long *a* sound:

ea as in *great*

ay as in *play*

a_e as in *take*

et as in *buffet*

eigh as in *eight*

a as in *table* (we called this the "lonely *a*," because *a* is "saying its name" without the help of any other vowel; this is also called an open syllable)

ie as in *lingerie* (okay, a group of teacher thought of this one during a workshop!)

And here are some of the ways we found to spell the long *e* sound:

ee as in *street*

e_e as in *theme*

y as in *baby*

ey as in *donkey*

ea as in *heat*

ie as in *believe*

e as in *enough* (the "lonely *e*")

i as in *ski*

Over a two-week period we collected hundreds of words that represent the long *e* and long *a* sound and were able to generalize about the most common ways to spell these sounds. (Clearly some patterns are more common than others.)

A "words about words" lesson

Students at the derivational relations stage need to explore word meanings and derivations. One way to launch word study at this level is by studying words about words. Begin by introducing the following words and have students find other words about words:

onomatopoeia (on-uh-mat-uh-PEE-uh); noun

The formation or use of words such as *buzz* or *murmur* that imitate the sounds associated with the objects or actions they refer to. (Why doesn't *onomatopoeia* sound the way it is?)

anagram (AN-a-gram); noun

A word or phrase formed by reordering the letters of another word or phrase, such as *satin* to *stain*. (Why isn't there another word that can be made by rearranging the letters of the word *anagram*?)

dyslexic (dis-LEK-sik); noun

A learning disorder marked by impairment of the ability to recognize and comprehend written words. (Why is *dyslexic* so difficult to read/spell?)

<u>mnemonic (ni-MON-ik); adjective</u>
Relating to, assisting, or intended to assist the memory. *Noun.* A device, such as a formula or rhyme, used as an aid in remembering. (Why is it so difficult to remember the spelling of the word *mnemonic*?)

<u>thesaurus (thi-SOR-uhs); noun</u>
A book of synonyms, often including related and contrasting words and antonyms.

<u>palindrome (PAL-in-droam); noun</u>
A word, phrase, verse, or sentence that reads the same backward or forward. For example: a man, a plan, a canal, Panama! (Why doesn't *palindrome* spell the same backward?)

Then spend time over a period of a few weeks collecting additional words about words. It takes many examples and lots of talk to get this subject started. You will be surprised at all the words students find.

Creating Conditions That Develop Students' Spelling Consciousness

Do you know people who always point out spelling mistakes in menus, books, newspapers, and newsletters? They're able to pick out the misspelled words wherever they go because they pay attention to spelling details and consequently have a high degree of spelling consciousness. As Marilyn vos Savant (2000) showed, this ability can be learned, and we can use a number of strategies to help students to develop this ability to notice when words are spelled incorrectly.

Recently I had an opportunity to work with a group of teachers in Atlanta. After I spent three days modeling how to run a writing workshop, we had a long discussion about the practical applications of what

I had modeled. The inevitable questions about how to teach spelling arose, so I asked them their personal beliefs about spelling. Although they all believed in allowing children to use invented spelling during drafts, they also had strong beliefs about the importance of correct spelling. As they said, we are all judged by the way that we spell, and when someone makes frequent spelling mistakes, we think of them as ignorant or uneducated. One teacher described it as only a Georgian can: "Poor spelling is like spinach in your teeth or walking out of the ladies room with your skirt tucked into your pantyhose." We all laughed and agreed. Invented spelling is fine for certain purposes, but if we let children publish misspelled work in our school publications and display it in our classrooms, we are sending a message that spelling does not really matter.

There are many games and activities that help students realize that correct spelling is not just something that strict teachers expect in school, that help them become excited about catching misspellings (see Appendix H).

One fifth-grade class I worked with developed a very high level of spelling consciousness after we noticed a spelling mistake in their district-produced spelling reference dictionary. The dictionary had the words *now* and *know* listed on the homophone page, but the example of correct usage next to them was, "I *now* you very well." As a group, the students then began looking for these "spelling bloopers." They started finding them everywhere: in student-made signs around the school, letters from the PTA, menus, newspapers, fliers, and advertisements.

When they went on a field trip to the nearby LegoLand amusement park, they couldn't wait to see me the next day to tell me about two mistakes they thought they had found on the LegoLand map. As it turns out, they were not misspellings, but they were still opportunities to talk about vocabulary. One was the phrase "tens of thousands of people visit each year." One student thought it should have said, "*tons* of thousands," but after some discussion, he understood that it wasn't an error. The second one was the name of a restaurant, *The Wok*. One of the students thought it was a misspelling of *walk*. Then another student realized that it was a restaurant. When they saw that the restaurant served egg rolls, another student piped up, "Oh, it's Chinese. It's the kind of *wok* you cook with." Now, tell me these kids weren't developing spelling consciousness and vocabulary!

They became so excited about finding misspellings that they came up with the idea of issuing spelling tickets, like speeding tickets. We looked at the language used on a real speeding ticket and modified it to produce our "spelling ticket" (see Figure 4–2). I told them they couldn't give each other tickets unless it was for a word on their portable word walls ("no excuses" words), because I didn't want them to be afraid to take risks in spelling. They decided to make a distinction between minor and major spelling errors, depending on whether the word was a real word in the wrong context or not even a word in our language. When one student remembered that when his dad got a speeding ticket he had to pay a fine, all the students wanted to know what the penalty would be for spelling tickets. After discussing it, we decided that it was embarrassing enough to have made a spelling mistake and have someone else catch it. A fifth grader coined the term "published humiliation"!

This class of "spelling police" caught their student teacher making so many spelling mistakes that they agreed not to write her a ticket if she corrected a mistake within thirty seconds of someone pointing it out. They made a bulletin board display in their classroom of all the tickets they'd issued and the misspellings they'd found.

One English professor at Burlington County College, in New Jersey, has had enough. If you visit his web page "OOOPS—Occasions of Proofreading Silliness" (http://staff.bcc.edu/jalexand/oops2.htm), you will see photographs he has taken of real-world spelling blunders, categorized by

Los Peñasquitos Elementary School
Spelling Police

Date: _____   Signature of Issuing Officer: _____

Ticket Issued to: _____

Offender's Signature: _____

▪▪▪

Reason for Spelling Violation:

▪▪▪

Type of Violation:

❏ Major: the misspelled word does not exist as a word in the English language.

❏ Minor: the misspelled word is a real word in our language. It is not the correct word in context.

▪▪▪

> **Location of Spelling Violation**
> ___ Newspaper _____
> ___ Magazine _____
> ___ Book _____
> ___ School Publication
> ___ Sign
> ___ Menu
> ___ Mail/Advertisement
> ___ Brochure or Flier
> ___ Map

Penalty: "PUBLISHED HUMILIATION"
This is a Warning Ticket!
To avoid penalty beyond "published humiliation"
Please fix this error in _____ days.

Figure 4–2. Los Peñasquitos Elementary School Spelling Ticket "degree of carelessness and the level of public accessibility." You can show this page to your students or at least tell the story and talk about some of the spelling errors that the professor has captured. Students are always intrigued by the notion that even adults make spelling mistakes, and that sometimes their misspellings have serious consequences.

Tools to develop students' spelling consciousness

In *Invitations* (1994), Regie Routman provides a list of questions to ask students about their spelling. These questions help build spelling consciousness because they turn the control over to the student. Students can also be taught to use these questions in peer conferences.

1. Which part looks right to you? (Put a check over the letters the student has used correctly.)

2. What else could you try?

3. What other letters could you use there to make the same sound?

4. What do you know about words that have the _____ sound at the end (for example, *er*)?

5. How else could you spell that?

6. You're missing a letter here (insert a caret where the letter is missing). What do you think it could be?

7. Do you know how to spell _____? This word has a part that's the same.

8. What spelling strategy could you try (assuming you've taught strategies)?

I also ask students who are stuck on a word to write it three different ways (I call this the "three tries" strategy) and then circle the one that looks right. Often, this simple technique produces the correctly spelled word or at least a closer, more developmentally appropriate approximation.

Do spell checkers help or hurt spelling consciousness?

Your students may try to tell you that spelling doesn't matter because there will always be a spell checker on their computers. Computer spell checkers are certainly tools to help spellers. But to a spell checker a word is a word; context is irrelevant. There are no misspellings in the following poem, but sense is another matter:

An Ode to the Spelling Chequer
Prays the Lord for the spelling chequer
That came with our pea sea!
Mecca mistake and it puts you rite
Its so easy to ewes, you sea.

I never used to no, was it e before eye?
(Four sometimes its eye before e.)
But now I've discovered the quay to success
It's as simple as won, too, free!

Sew watt if you lose a letter or two,
The whirled won't come two an end!
Can't you sea? It's as plane as the knows on yore face
S. Chequer's my very best friend.

I've always had trubble with letters that double
"Is it one or to S's?" I'd wine
But now, as I've tolled you this chequer is grate
And its hi thyme you got won, like mine.

—Anonymous

Communicating with Parents About Your Methods

It is very important to let parents know about your spelling program so that they can understand, feel included in, and reinforce the excitement that the children are experiencing. If the parents become interested, they can engage in some of these activities at home, playing spelling police on car trips, using flash cards for high frequency words, and so on. (See Appendix K for more ideas about activities for parents and caregivers.) Some of the issues to be addressed specifically with parents are:

- Weekly spelling tests.
- Uses and misuses of spell checkers on the computer.
- Stages of development (best explained at parent conferences).

Caregivers have an important role to play in memorizing high frequency words. Here is a letter I sent home with the third graders I was working with, along with a list of high frequency words ("no excuses words") to be studied and memorized:

> Dear Parents and Caregivers,
>
> Enclosed is a list of high frequency words that all third graders are expected to know. Also in this envelope are study cards (flash cards) of your child's "personal words" (words your child tends to misspell) that need to be learned at home. They should be studied as a homework task until mastered. We will be retesting students for these words next month.
>
> Thank you,
> Mrs. Marten

I printed this letter on the outside of an envelope and had a parent volunteer make the flash cards to put inside.

Figure 4–3 is the letter I sent home after I began word study with this group of third graders. (This was before we started the new spelling approach in our district. They had finished our district's spelling program and their teacher was looking for more activities to do for the remainder of the year.) This letter shows you how to invite caregivers to enter into the spirit of the word-crafting lessons, and it familiarizes them with your method, outlining the four components/goals: (1) learning spelling strategies, (2) memorizing high frequency words, (3) learning common patterns, and (4) developing spelling consciousness.

Dear Parents,

You will hear us talk a lot about word study in third grade. Mr. Sandstrom and I are working together to teach your child far more about spelling than basic memorization. As you will see, memorizing words is just one part of our word study. We are also studying about letters, sounds, patterns, and meanings of words.

We have four main goals for our word-study program:

1. Students will learn spelling strategies that will assist them when they are trying to spell unfamiliar words. I want your child to be able to rely on "sounding it out" as only *one* of several strategies. Some of the other strategies I will teach are using references, asking a more expert speller, three tries, sounds like, and looks like.

2. Students will learn how to memorize words. I will teach them which words should be memorized. Expecting students to memorize every word just doesn't work. However, there are key "accountability words," very common words that are used in everyday writing. You received a list of these words in an earlier letter. We will continue to send regular updates about your child's progress in memorizing these words. These words can be studied like the multiplication tables; they just need to be memorized and spelled correctly all the time. We have many classroom resources available, including our class word wall, our class "word plus" dictionary, and our portable word wall. After studying and correcting the spelling of these words enough times, your child will learn them!

3. Students will learn common patterns used in spelling. Third graders typically are ready to learn the various long vowel patterns. Much of our word study will begin with an examination of the various long vowel patterns. For example, when we do a word study about long *a* patterns we will explore and discover the following long *a* patterns: s**a**m**e**, p**ai**n, pl**ay**, **eigh**t.

4. Students will develop a "spelling consciousness." I expect your child to become a word expert. As we explore words through spelling and meaning, your child will begin to develop a curiosity and interest in words that will carry over into reading and other academic areas. We will become more aware of words and patterns, and students will begin to find "spelling bloopers" in newspapers, menus, advertisements, and school publications (unfortunately, it happens!). They have already developed a "spelling ticket" to issue to anyone who is "caught" making a spelling mistake.

If you have any questions about our word-study lessons in third grade, do not hesitate to call me. Also, feel free to stop by our class during word-study time. It is usually every day from 1:15–2:00. Just check with Mr. Sandstrom in the morning to be sure there hasn't been a change in the schedule.

Sincerely,

Cindy Marten
Literacy Specialist

Figure 4–3. Parent Letter to Introduce Word Study

Professional Responsibility

Teachers can approach spelling instruction in a systematic, logical, and sequential manner; but if that instruction is divorced from our current knowledge about the developmental stages of learners, the results are weak. As part of my research I often interview other teachers informally about how they teach spelling and vocabulary. The range of responses is intriguing. Some teachers say they don't teach spelling at all or that their district doesn't have a spelling program. Of those who do use a program, many say they use the Sitton Spelling Sourcebook program. Other teachers approach spelling from a linguistic perspective with a predetermined scope and sequence of memorization and phonics skills to be covered at a particular grade level and during a particular school year.

Clearly, the key to effective teaching is twofold:

1. Understand spelling development; make it your professional responsibility to develop an understanding of how spelling develops and the predictable developmental phases most children pass through on their way to conventional spelling.

2. Understand your children as developing spellers. What should you teach? You'll know if you observe your students; collect their writing samples; talk with them; and get a clear sense of what they know about spelling and what they need to know.

In this way, your teaching will become both smart and targeted. You'll be able to help your students at their point of need. Embrace these two professional challenges and you'll be on your way to *teaching* spelling (no more simplistic assigning and correcting!). Figure 4–4 sums up some essential practices.

(*Adapted from a handout that was part of a Words Your Way conference in Reno, Nevada*)

Social Interaction

Work to move what students know about words and spelling from a tacit to an explicit level by creating contexts for social interaction.

Experiences with Sorting Words and Letters

Give students opportunities to think about patterns and relationships by having them sort words and letters. Skillful questioning will help them develop critical thinking as they look for similarities and differences in words. They will begin to compare and contrast words and discover the patterns. **Always use words they can read.** Picture sorts are necessary for our youngest students who are learning about sounds, but can't independently read enough words to extend their knowledge about sounds.

Flexible Grouping

Remember that your students may move through the first three stages quickly. (The last two stages last a lifetime.) Continually reassess your students to stay on top of their increasing knowledge.

Word Study Games

Use games to review knowledge, not to teach new information.

Personal Record Keeping

Have students keep word-crafting notebooks throughout the year as a record of their growing linguistic knowledge.

Use Words Students Can Read

For all word-crafting activities, use words the students can read fluently out of context.

Figure 4–4. Essential Practices in Teaching Spelling

Know Your Spelling Tools

Consumer Beware

Certainly teachers should talk to each other about their practice; indeed, one of the serious flaws of school structure is to give teachers virtually no professional time for such collaboration. But if such talk is limited to the exchange of gimmicks or recipes for teaching, little improvement and no substantial difference in educational practice is likely to result. Change can only be made possible if teachers explore together not only whether a particular activity works; but what it works for, for whom, and why it does so. For it is only through exploring and reflecting on the whys of practice, which are more or less explicit theories, that we can develop the underlying knowledge we need to understand the essence of a particular activity. And we must understand its essence if we are to be able to adapt it successfully to our own classroom context, and, perhaps most crucially, to evaluate its effectiveness in terms of pupil learning.

—*John Mayher*

Once you have a fundamental understanding of spelling's developmental stages, you are ready to identify a stage and then the linguistic features that children typically are ready to explore at each stage. However, this underlying knowledge by itself isn't all you need. This book has presented the principles of effective spelling instruction, but you are the only one who can decide which tools you need and when to use them. If you watch your students carefully, you will make smart decisions about the right resources to have in your tool cabinet.

As teachers, we have thousands of tools at our disposal. Some are basic ones, the simple hammer and nails that all teachers use: pencils, paper, crayons, software, games, workbooks, curriculum guides, standards. However, as we all know, simply having these tools doesn't in any way ensure that our students will learn what they need to know. Even if we have all of the tools needed to build a bookshelf, we will never be able to produce a bookshelf until we have lots of experience and know exactly which tools to use and how to use them.

Remember the days when your old Dolch word game was brand-new and fresh out of the box? You had all your students play it, even though you didn't know or care whether they needed to play it. That traditional way of teaching reminds me of the expression, "If all you have is a hammer, then everything begins to look like a nail." Since we now have so many more "hammers," we have to be even more selective and purposeful in our use of word study games and resources. Nevertheless, you may find yourself returning to some old tools you thought you would never use again. With your emerging understanding of developmental spelling and the linguistic elements of print, a dusty old phonics game may have a specific purpose for a student who is stuck or may be used to launch a specific inquiry into a feature or sound you want to study.

In California, where I teach, we have been given a mandate to include "direct, systematic, explicit phonics" in our teaching. Naturally, the educational materials publishers and suppliers glommed on to that mandate and started mass-producing and stocking phonics games galore. We need to be cautious consumers of these products, not fooled by the glitz. Some are very expensive, and most are not necessary. The way I see it, the tools are only as good as the craftsperson. My aim is to help you know what tools are available and what they can do for you.

My husband spent years in a research lab, and he often talks about his assistant, who always seemed to know which tool he needed before he needed it. I may not be able to be at your side handing you the exact tool, but I can promise you that if you take inventories, analyze student writing, and give your students multiple opportunities to write, you will choose tools that help your students learn to spell.

In Chapter 2, I build a case for making the teaching of spelling (word crafting or word study) as fine a craft as possible. Traditional teachers tend to focus exclusively on the linguistic elements of the written language. Although we certainly need to be knowledgeable about the linguistic features of print, that knowledge is only valuable in so far as it helps us understand the miscues in the spelling (or encoding) of our students. As Richard Gentry points out (see Chapter 3), we have to attend to what the child is thinking at each stage and use that to inform our practice. The concrete evidence of their thinking is in the spelling.

Selecting Your Tools

I had just finished presenting a full-day inservice on effective spelling instruction, and a teacher rushed up to talk to me. With a twinkle in her eye, she put a loving, grandmotherly hand on my shoulder. "It's so good to see that bright young teachers like you are finally starting to realize that we have to teach phonics. I was so tired of all that whole language nonsense. I had to hide my worksheets when my principal came into my room. But, after hearing you talk today, I know I don't have to hide them anymore. I've been teaching long enough to know that it would come back in style again."

Oh my goodness, I thought, what have I done! I frantically replayed what I might have said that day that gave her permission to drag out dusty old phonics worksheets and wave them in her principal's face with my handout and email address to back her up. I realized that in my presentation I had talked about phonics—diphthongs, blends, digraphs, short and long vowels, prefixes and suffixes, terms this woman had probably not heard in professional conversations for over ten years. Now she was hearing them again, and her principal had even paid for her to come to my workshop. She was ecstatic, but she had missed the point of my presentation. She cared more about particular tools than she did about particular students.

"Finally, someone in this district has some sense again," she said. She asked me to follow her to her classroom so she could show me the worksheets and workbooks that she had been using secretly. She told me that when she tried to order the books several years ago the district had denied her request, so she was using her own money to run off copies. It made up her entire word-study curriculum. She was certain that after my presentation she would be able to submit her purchase order to her principal and it would be approved. It was actually a pretty good workbook, an excellent resource for teaching Greek and Latin roots and derivatives. I wrote down the title and ordered one for myself; and I will use it, not as a stand-alone program, but only as a resource for students who are in the derivational relations stage.

I am, however, glad that my presentation empowered that teacher to articulate a clear rationale and philosophical pedagogy to support her use of those materials. Since her principal also attended my session, I hope that they will be able to reexamine her teaching resource and make some professional decisions about where it fits into the developmental sequence of her students while still addressing the district standards.

Walk into any teacher supply store and you will see the hundreds of tools, gizmos, gadgets, games, and workbooks now available for teaching spelling. In fact, if you've been teaching long enough, your own supply cabinets might be filled with some old "phonics games" that you had to put away in the late 1980s and early 1990s. (Some principals went so far as threaten that if they saw one phonics game or worksheet out during language arts class, you would be written up.) Well, maybe you can dust off those old games. It might be safe to bring them out again; but not because that principal has retired, and not just because the National Reading Panel has spoken and declared that phonics is now the most effective way to teach children to read. No, the only acceptable reason to drag out some of those old phonics games and activities is that you are now armed with a new instructional context and developmental framework that will make the work relevant to the students and be connected to authentic reading and writing.

If you are a relatively new teacher, you are in different circumstances. In some ways, you need to be even more cautious about the tools you select. When I walked into a popular teaching supply store in September of this year, I was shocked at how many "word study" and "phonics" products were on the shelves. As I said, the educational suppliers and publishers have tried to exploit the "phonics phrenzy" that is sweeping reading education. They are making the games and worksheets faster than we can spend our hard-earned salaries on them. Many of them are largely unnecessary. In one store, I counted 158 different products, including games, flash cards, workbooks, activity packs, puppets, balls, and tiles, all promising to teach your students the all-important phonics.

Please know that I am in no way opposed to any one of these 158 products. They may be excellent products—but we, as teachers, need to be cautious consumers of them. Patrick Shannon even wrote a book called *iSHOP You Shop* (2001) in which he warns teachers not to get drawn into the market exploitation of teacher supplies. *iSHOP You Shop* is a guide to becoming a savvy consumer; it tells you how to spot a lemon, and it addresses why we desire to buy reading commodities in the first place. Shopping has become so quick and easy that we now have little time to think about *what* we buy and *why* we buy it. Whether it be phonics programs, test prep kits, or bulletin board borders, everywhere we turn, someone is trying to sell us something that promises to improve our teaching.

Consider yourself warned, and then walk into (or log on to the website of) a teaching supply store with purpose and caution. Be armed with the knowledge of exactly what you need, and base those needs on close observation of your students. Make sure that you have set up daily opportunities for them to read and write for sustained amounts of time. Then you will not waste your money on tools you don't need, and may even be a better teacher.

A final caveat. Just because I have listed a resource in this book does not mean it is the right tool for you or, more important, for your student. I've found all of these tools to have some merit and value in a word-study classroom. But it would be a horrible mistake for you to order every single one of them in your quest to be a strong word-crafting teacher. Build your toolbox carefully. Be selective. Be smart about what you are buying. Remember, it's not the tools that determine the quality and effectiveness of your word-crafting classroom. It's the instructional context. Setting up word-crafting contexts means connecting the study of words to authentic reading and writing.

Appendices

Appendix A
Spelling Pilot Adoption—Evaluation of Publisher Materials

Publisher/Series	_____ Teacher
	_____ Administrator
_____	_____ Parent

Please circle one score in response to each question.

PROGRAM DESCRIPTION   **SCORE**

1. Is this series based on a clear <u>developmental continuum</u>? For example, does the instructional sequence for grades 1–8 represent the stages of spelling development over time?

   Low   1   2   3   4   5   High   x 1.5 = _____

2. Does this series provide multilevel word lists based on <u>linguistic patterns</u> (sound, pattern, meaning)? For example, grades 1 and 2 will predominantly address sound; grades 3 and 4, pattern; grades 5–8, meaning.

   Low   1   2   3   4   5   High   x 1.5 = _____

3. Does this series offer a variety of instructional materials and practices to meet the different <u>spelling stages within one classroom</u>? For example, strategies support students at within-word pattern, syllable juncture, etc.

   Low   1   2   3   4   5   High   x 1.5 = _____

4. Does this series provide teachers with suggestions for applying spelling strategies within the <u>context of the curriculum</u>? For example, students are asked to compose a paragraph on a topic of study and incorporate current spelling patterns.

   Low   1   2   3   4   5   High   _____

5. Does this series address <u>high frequency words</u> and memorization? For example, in what order are sight words introduced?

   Low   1   2   3   4   5   High   _____

6. Does this series provide a variety of tools/strategies to meet diagnostic, ongoing, and post<u>assessment</u> needs?

   Low   1   2   3   4   5   High   _____

7. Would you consider this series to be well organized, easy to implement, and <u>easy to manage</u>? For example, is the teacher's manual easy to follow?

   Low   1   2   3   4   5   High   x 1.5 = _____

8. Does this series include activities that are <u>interactive and motivating</u> for students? For example, games, word sorts, and puzzles.

   Low   1   2   3   4   5   High   _____

9. Is this series aligned to <u>district standards</u> across grade levels? For example, see standards.

   Low   1   2   3   4   5   High   _____

10. Does this series provide support for strengthening <u>home/school communication</u> and parent partnership at home? For example, is there recommended homework with explanations for parents?

    Low   1   2   3   4   5   High   _____

TOTAL SCORE: _____

NOTE: More "weight" was given to questions 1, 2, 3, and 7 because of their importance.

Comments:

Appendix B
Innovation Configuration Rubric for Effective Spelling Instruction

Circle the description that most closely describes your current practice.

	4	3	2	1
COMPONENT 1 ASSESSMENT FOR DIAGNOSIS	Ongoing multiple assessments of developmental stages	Assessment of developmental stages to begin year	Administration of Houghton Mifflin pretest at beginning of year	No administration of diagnostic assessment
COMPONENT 2 MEETING STUDENT NEEDS	Each student engaged in learning activities at appropriate developmental level	Some students engaged in differentiated learning activities at their appropriate developmental level	All students engaged in learning activities at same developmental level	
COMPONENT 3 INSTRUCTIONAL CONTEXT	Spelling is taught as a tool for effective and purposeful written communication	Spelling is taught and practiced with limited application to writing	Spelling is assigned with limited application to writing	Spelling is assigned with no application to writing
COMPONENT 4 TEACHING CONCEPTS (sounds/patterns/meaning)	Study of words based on sounds/patterns/meanings	Study of words based on high frequency usage and/or common misspellings	Study of thematic or vocabulary-based word lists	Study of random word lists
COMPONENT 5 TEACHING HIGH FREQUENCY WORDS	Appropriate instruction *and* accountability for frequency words	Some instruction *and* accountability for high frequency words	Some instruction *or* accountability for high frequency words	No instruction or accountability for high frequency words
COMPONENT 6 INSTRUCTIONAL IMPLEMENTATION	Students are actively engaged in a variety of activities to build understanding of spelling	Students participate in a limited variety of activities to discover spelling generalizations	Students are assigned rules and words to memorize	Students are assigned words to memorize
COMPONENT 7 ASSESSMENT FOR ACCOUNTABILITY	Ongoing multiple assessments to evaluate student progress	Regular posttests of words that fit the spelling generalization	Weekly posttests of list words	No assessment for spelling accountability

Appendix C
Case Study Exercise for Innovation Configurations for Effective Spelling Instruction

(Use the Innovation Configuration Matrix to give each teacher a score)

TEACHER	Component 1 Assessment for Diagnosis	Component 2 Meeting Student Needs	Component 3 Instructional Context	Component 4 Teaching Concepts	Component 5 High Frequency Words	Component 6 Instructional Implications	Component 7 Assessment for Accountability
Wanda							
Fred							
Sally							
Lydia							
Victor							

Teacher A

Wanda Word-Study

Wanda is in her second year of teaching. She has taught the same grade level both years and is well liked by her students. She is still somewhat overwhelmed by all that teaching requires. She likes the Houghton Mifflin spelling materials and is attempting to teach each unit and all of the lessons within each unit.

In order to cut down on the logistic challenge of differentiating her instruction, she has chosen to provide spelling instruction for her whole class in daily lessons. She supports her spelling strugglers and extends her spelling superstars with appropriate questioning throughout each lesson. Follow-up activities vary based on the needs of each student. Additional support for strugglers is provided during reading group instruction and through at-home practice.

Wanda administered the Houghton Mifflin diagnostic pretest at the beginning of the year. It helped her recognize which of her students would need additional support and which students would need extension work. She emphasizes accurate spelling of lesson words in daily spelling work and on weekly tests.

Teacher B

Fred Flex

Fred's classroom is often in what appears to be chaos, students and materials are everywhere, and Fred may be anywhere. Traditionally, however, his students have consistently achieved excellent assessment results and have outperformed students in other classrooms.

Fred is a veteran teacher who has experience with skills-based mastery teaching, individualized teaching, and whole language teaching. He is now quite at home with what he sees as a sensible balance between all approaches.

Fred is teaching all of the Houghton Mifflin units and enhancing them with his extensive background knowledge and experience. He has become particularly intrigued with the developmental spelling levels and is working to align his instruction with his students' developmental levels. He teaches learning activities and strategies (e.g., word sorts) to his whole class, then works with small homogeneous groups to apply the strategies to word lists of appropriate complexity. All students generally complete the textbook activities for homework; the assignments vary in length based on students' developmental level. He also requires weekly practice with high frequency words for all students.

At the beginning of the year, Fred administered both the Houghton Mifflin diagnostic assessment and a phonetic spelling inventory to all students. He also assessed mastery of high frequency words over the course of the first two weeks. To monitor student progress, he checks high frequency word accuracy in students' writing, administers biweekly spelling pattern assessments comprising ten random words that exemplify the pattern being studied, and evaluates cumulative progress with the Houghton Mifflin unit review tests.

Teacher C

Sally Spelling

Sally is also her site's English language learners coordinator and was unable to attend the August inservice because of a scheduling conflict. She has distributed the Houghton Mifflin textbooks to her students, but they have not yet used them. Her teacher materials are stacked behind her desk, also as yet unopened.

Sally places heavy emphasis on phonetic features and chooses to continue using the worksheets and tests she has used in past years. Her students receive weekly spelling lists, daily worksheets, and regular practice activities for homework. She also adds five words from the district accountability word lists to each week's word list. All work is completed independently in class or at home. Sally has been known to say, "Good spellers are born spellers."

Sally gives weekly spelling tests and records the percentage correct for each student in her grade book. She began her spelling program during the second week of school with all students receiving the same word lists and assignments. She did not see a need to preassess her students.

Teacher D

Lydia Letters

Lydia is very enthusiastic about the Houghton Mifflin materials and the information she learned as a member of last year's steering committee. She also participated as a pilot teacher last spring.

Lydia has become a strong believer in the validity of teaching students at their developmental levels. As a result, she bases her instructional plan on generalized spelling strategies, developmental stages, and application in writing. Her students use the Houghton Mifflin textbooks and activities regularly to practice the linguistic features they are studying. Materials from the grade levels before and after the grade level Lydia teaches are in evidence in her classroom. Students regularly look for and record similar-pattern words from their independent reading books. They receive "bonus points" for using pattern words in any of their written work. Lydia meets with homogeneous groups of students two or three times each week. Students working below grade level meet more frequently than the others.

Lydia has enlisted the support of her students' parents to assist with mastery of high frequency and commonly misspelled words. Students are expected to practice daily by selecting from a list of suggested practice activities that Lydia distributed at Back-to-School Night. She monitors mastery by assessing accuracy in written work and by scoring pop quizzes made up of a random selection of grade-level "no excuses" words.

To begin the year, Lydia spent three weeks teaching learning activities (e.g., word sorts) and graphic organizers (e.g., word ladders) to all her students using words representative of the previous grade level. She then administered both the Houghton Mifflin diagnostic test and a phonetic spelling inventory to each student. She continues to monitor progress with biweekly pattern tests. She plans to readminister the spelling inventory at midyear and at the end of the year.

Teacher E

Victor Vocabulary

Victor is one of the most senior faculty members. He plans to retire in a couple years. He has already covered many of the Houghton Mifflin lessons and says there is not enough content for a full school year, largely because the words are too easy. He also advocates using vocabulary word lists for spelling practice.

Victor has an extensive vocabulary program that he has used for many years. Students are held accountable for learning fifteen challenging vocabulary words each week. They are assigned independent worksheets, weekly sentences, and at-home practice tests. Students take a weekly test that includes accurately spelling each word and providing its definition. As well as using the Houghton Mifflin materials this year, Victor is also assigning weekly spelling lists, textbook activities, and Friday tests using the word lists from the Houghton Mifflin series.

Appendix D
Teacher References and Resources for Effective Word Study

Work on building your teacher resource library to help build your knowledge of word study. Your school may want to begin a collection of teacher resources that are most helpful. This list contains some that I have found most useful. There are many, many more helpful books and articles. When we first started our study in my district, we collected a series of excellent articles that we wanted each teacher to read (see Chapter 2), and we made them available in a binder at each school site. You might start by collecting some key articles to help start conversations about effective spelling instruction.

Words Their Way: Word Study for Phonics, Vocabulary, and Spelling Instruction, by Donald R. Bear, Marcia Invernizzi, Shane Templeton, and Francine Johnston

Your word-study resource library begins with this book. It is an essential resource for effective spelling instruction; it will teach you the principles of developmental spelling instruction. An extensive section on games and activities is provided, and it is sequenced by developmental stage. There is a third edition, released in May 2003, that includes significant changes, among them updated spelling inventories, strengthened upper-grade materials, a free CD, added English-language-learner components, and more games and activities for every developmental level. You can also order a sixty-seven-minute video of classroom word study lessons. All of the file-folder games found in *Words Their Way* can now be purchased from Marian Clish (www.writers-marketplace.com). Also, every summer there is Words Your Way Conference in Reno. I highly recommend attending; classroom visits and lectures by Donald Bear and Shane Templeton are highlights. You will leave with a suitcase full of ideas and information. For more information go to www.unr.edu/cll and click on the Word Study Workshop icon.

The Spelling Teacher's Book of Lists, by Jo Phenix

Memorizing the spelling of all the words we use is impossible! This practical book will help you to improve your students' spelling skills and encourage them to use pattern recognition, meaning, and problem solving, rather than trying to rely solely on their memorization. The lists focus on consonants, vowels, confusing spellings, linguistic roots, and useful rules. Numerous notes about regional variations, etymology, and exceptions, as well as pertinent teaching and spelling tips, provide a wealth of opportunities for capitalizing on "teachable moments."

Word Journeys: Assessment-Guided Phonics, Spelling, and Vocabulary Instruction, by Kathy Ganske

This book presents a highly practical approach to assessing children's spelling ability and word knowledge, and to offering effective, appropriate instruction. Included is a dictated word inventory that enables teachers to quickly and easily evaluate students' stages of spelling development and their knowledge of important orthographic features. It sets forth detailed guidelines for engaging students in hands-on word study, and it is tailored to their specific strengths and weaknesses. Particularly useful features of the book include narrative "snapshots" of children at different stages of spelling development; numerous examples of student work; suggested word sort activities for each orthographic feature; lists of recommended books and poems; and a focus on fostering a love of words through word play and language appreciation. The appendix includes blackline masters and a list of over 12,000 words, arranged by sound, pattern, and meaning-related features.

Basic Skills Series: Spelling Grades 1–6, by Roberta Bodensteiner, Series Editor (Instructional Fair, Grand Rapids, MI)

These are workbooks, plain and simple. Some of my colleagues asked me to find a resource that has worksheets for students who are doing independent practice or homework. I have looked at many, many spelling workbooks and practice sheets, and this is one of the best. What I like about this series is that the linguistic features presented at each grade level are developmentally aligned to what you expect students to be studying at that grade. For example, the first-grade book has activities and word lists that cover the common letter name features (short vowels and blends). It also has within-word features (the basic long-vowel patterns) that are appropriate for some first graders. The fourth-grade book addresses short and long vowels for older students who still may be using but confusing these patterns, but the words are more sophisticated so students won't feel they are doing "baby work." Each section also includes a writing component. Another good thing: these books are only $5.99 each! My only criticism is a very small one and has nothing to do with the content. The bee on the cover of each workbook is holding the same word list no matter the grade level, and the words on the list don't follow a linguistic pattern. Clearly, the cover artist doesn't understand how to teach spelling; luckily, Roberta Bodensteiner, the editor of the series, does.

All Sorts of Sorts: Word Sorts for Reinforcing Spelling and Phonetic Patterns, by Sheron Brown

This book will help your students categorize the visual features of words. Words are sorted by initial and final consonants, vowel patterns, blends, phonograms, and more. The one hundred and fifty-five word sorts in this book are an excellent way to present students with reinforcement and additional word study practice in large-group, small-group, individual, and learning-center settings. They foster a multisensory approach that allows students to sort, manipulate, and categorize words in various ways, including open, closed, speed, blind, and writing sorts.

All Sorts of Sorts 2: Word Sorts for Complex Spelling & Phonetic Pattern Reinforcement, by Sheron Brown

Ready-to-use, classroom-tested, developmental word sorts! Sheron Brown has written a word-sorting book that will challenge your intermediate- and upper-grade students. Word sorting is a basic word study activity that asks students to group words according to categories. *All Sorts of Sorts 2* presents spelling rules, word and phonics patterns, and spelling generalizations in a unique format that challenges students to sort the words within categories. The book contains one hundred and seventy word sorts reflecting the types of spelling and phonics principles that intermediate- to upper-grade students encounter in their daily reading and written work. The five types of word sorts are explained, and detailed instructions on how to have your students do them are included. Additional word-sorting activities are explained, and there are blank word sort blackline masters for the teacher who wishes to create her own.

Spelling Development Disability and Instruction, by Louisa Moats

Since I'm not a linguistic, I had to turn to Dr. Moats and others to teach me about the linguistic elements of our language. What I appreciate about Dr. Moats' book is that she places the linguistic elements of the language in the context of how children develop. She has worked to help teachers understand phonics for the simple reason that she believes we need to understand more than we do about how our spelling system works. She has put together comprehensive training sessions to introduce teachers to linguistics. I also attended one of her LETRS (Language Essentials for Teachers of Reading and Spelling, Sopris West, Longmont, CO) workshops. In a three-day seminar I learned more about the particular linguistic elements of our language than I had learned in all my schooling. Moats has also generously given her time and expertise in answering so many, many questions I had while I was learning with my students. She has just published a spelling program with Sopris West called *Spellography.*

"Using Students' Invented Spellings as a Guide for Spelling Instruction That Emphasizes Word Study," by Marcia A. Invernizzi, M. P. Abouzeid, and J. T. Gill

This article outlines a theory of developmental spelling that evolved from research on children's invented spellings. It shows teachers when best to teach different aspects of spelling and provides examples and several minilessons to show how words are examined by sound, by within-word patterns, and by meaning.

"Robin, Owl, Eeyore, and Nvntd Splling," by Pat Timberlake

This article examines invented spelling as a stage of progress in children's writing growth. It suggests that children generally understand consonant sounds first, then begin using invented spelling, often omitting all or most vowels. Gradually, as children make the transition to conventional spelling, vowels are added. Also proposes ways to facilitate children's natural writing development.

WordWorks: Exploring Language Play, by Bonnie von Hoff Johnson (Fulcrum Resources)

A resource filled with word play for students at later developmental stages. "A delightful compendium of information about wordplay. With an entertaining style, Johnson gives background on puns, idioms, proverbs, and other examples of language play. Books and activities to explore the topics are included. Her informative and entertaining style makes this ideal for general reading in addition to teachers of grades 4–8."

The Great Word Catalogue: FUNdamental Activities for Building Vocabulary, by Susan Ohanian (Heinemann)

Quite a collection of everything you need to know to be able to play with language and engage in explorations to take you to the wonderful world of words. "In her inimitable way, Susan Ohanian offers something new and different to use in the classroom. She brings language to life in this irresistible invitation to investigate vocabulary, to practice and play with words. At once whimsical and functional, *The Great Word Catalogue: FUNdamental Activities for Building Vocabulary* delivers on its title, showing teachers and students that fundamentals are fun and that fun is fundamental." The Word Watch, Word Challenge, and Word Puzzler features, the Teaching Tips, and reproducible activities are immediately doable.

Richard Lederer

Mr. Lederer is a self-proclaimed Verbivore. His many books about the English language will come in handy in your word-crafting classroom as he knows how to work with words in ways you seldom see. His books are too many to list and his website is worth exploring to find out more about his books and his lifelong interest in words. He even hosts a Sunday program called *A Way with Words* on the local PBS radio station. His website is www.verbivore.com.

Teaching Kids to Spell, by J. Richard Gentry and Jean Wallace Gillet (Heinemann)

Teaching Kids to Spell fills the need for a book to help teachers provide systematic, personalized spelling instruction in an integrated language arts program. The authors provide a much-needed bridge between traditional spelling instruction and whole language approaches. It shows teachers (and parents, too) how spelling ability begins to emerge in young children's invented spellings, how it grows as children pass through predictable stages of spelling strategies, and how eventually every student can reach a standard of correct "expert" spelling. The text includes word lists, tips for teaching predictable patterns, and a variety of individual activities that prepare children to meet the phonetic, semantic, historical, and visual demands of spelling; it also includes strategies for implementing a spelling workshop in the elementary classroom.

Spelling Instruction That Makes Sense, by Jo Phenix and Doreen Scott-Dunne (Pembroke)

This groundbreaking book dispels the myths and misconceptions that surround the teaching of spelling. Full of practical ideas for K–6 classrooms, the book presents teaching strategies that will help students explore the fun and structure of language as they gain experience and confidence in their writing. It includes fascinating facts about spelling, phonics, and language and a thorough analysis of evaluation and record keeping.

Learning to Read and Spell: The Child's Knowledge of Words, by Edmund H. Henderson (Northern Illinois University Press)

You really have to have at least one book by the man I consider the father of word study: Edmund Henderson. In all I've learned about developmental spelling, Henderson's name seems to crop up each time. This book is a good overview to his work.

Spelling In Use: Looking Closely at Spelling in Whole Language Classrooms, by Lester Laminack and Katie Wood (National Council of Teachers of English)

In accessible and lively prose, Laminack and Wood describe both the theoretical foundations and the practical details of whole language classrooms, where learning to spell occurs in the context of purposeful writing. A rich collection of student writing is presented and analyzed in detail, which makes the book exceptionally valuable for inservice discussions or workshops on spelling and writing instruction. The book also includes chapters designed to help teachers include parents, and it offers responses to frequently asked questions from parents and administrators.

What's a Schwa Sound Anyway? by Sandra Wilde (Heinemann)

A very helpful introduction to linguistics, with an exploration of how we learn to read, spell, and pronounce words. Answers the questions, Why are some words hard to spell? What are the best ways for kids—and adults—to figure out unfamiliar words?

You Kan Red This! by Sandra Wilde (Heinemann)

This is the book that really started my quest for better spelling instruction. As I re-read this book recently I realized that it has so much in it to help word-crafting teachers. It is filled with minilessons, spelling strategies, and useful information. My copy is dog-eared and has notes all over it. It is probably the most helpful book I have on my shelf in terms of practical, smart information about spelling instruction. Sandra Wilde helped me rethink my approach to spelling with this book way before I ever heard of spelling inventories or developmental stages. *You Kan Red This!* is a comprehensive handbook for K–6 teachers that answers questions like these: How can I integrate spelling and punctuation into writing? How do I know if my students are learning and improving? Can (or should) I throw out the spelling books? How can I show that invented spelling works? When, if ever, should I tell kids how to spell words? Are there ways to focus on spelling and punctuation that won't be boring?

Dictionaries and Word Reference Books

The standard dictionary will quickly prove inadequate when you truly create a class full of students intrigued by words. They will want as many references as you can find. Start with one or two. I suggest looking at some of these to give you an idea of what's available. A good way to find more is to go to Amazon.com and enter in one of these titles. You will see many more links to similar books that might be helpful for your class.

The Dictionary of Word Origins, by John Ayto

The average English speaker knows approximately 50,000 words—almost 25 times more words than there are stars visible in the night sky. This book uncovers the often surprising connections between words. In more than 8,000 entries, the dictionary reveals the origins of and links between words like *beef* and *cow*, *secret* and *crime, flour* and *pollen, imbecile* and *bacteria, plankton* and *complain*. Written in a clear and informative style, *The Dictionary of Word Origins* shows how English today has developed from its Indo-European origins and how diverse influences on the language have intermingled.

The Merriam-Webster New Book of Word Histories

A gold mine of fascinating word histories! This engaging and informative book reveals the origins of 1,500 words, from *abigail* to *zombie,* from the mythology of ancient Greece to the comic strips of the 20th century. You will discover how a skimpy bathing suit came to be called a *bikini* and what *serendipity* has to do with Horace Walpole.

Word Stems: A Dictionary, by John Kennedy

This is a classic reference handbook for students of the English language. It uses the cores, or stems, of words to define and decipher the most commonly used foreign words that form the foundation of our English words (our language is a hybrid of Latin, Greek and some ten other languages). *Word Stems* is perfect for students, word buffs, puzzlers, and writers.

The Concise Oxford Dictionary of English Etymology, by T. F. Hoad

With over 17,000 entries, this is the most authoritative and comprehensive guide to word origins available in paperback. It contains a wealth of information about our language and its history. For example, readers will learn that *bungalow* originally meant belonging to Bengal, that *assassin* comes from the Arabic for hashish-eater, and that *nice* meant foolish or stupid in the thirteenth century, coy or shy in the fifteenth. And *adder, anger,* and *umpire* were originally spelled with an initial *n*.

The Synonym Finder, by J. I. Rodale

Everyone who works with words will welcome this magnificent aid to finding the ever-elusive "right" word. Many of the reviews at Amazon.com mention that this book is even better and more useful than a thesaurus.

21st Century Synonym and Antonym Finder, edited by Barbara Ann Kipfer

This is a guide to more than 20,000 synonyms and antonyms, in an easy-to-use, A-to-Z format. It uses modern preferred usages and spellings, avoids outmoded, useless entries, and includes such added features as headword definitions.

Long Ē

ea		ee		lonely e	Y at the end
beam	teach	street	eel	zebra	Polly	Patty
leap	leach	creepy	sheet	even	dolly	Daddy
bean	beanie babie	wheel	beet	being	money	Janurary
steal	speak	keep	greedy	behind	tummy	February
reap	beak	sleep	coffee	we		every
mean	beat	weep	week	he		bunny
steam	each	weed	agreed	began		plenty
stream	hear	reed	feed	because		any
bead	clear	speed	sleeves	he		only
neat	weak	need	wee	be		fifty
treat	near	teeth	cheek	median		sixty
clean	neat	steed				twenty
lead	leave	tree		enormous		seventy
squeal	sea	see		beside		eighty
meat	easily	three		people		ninety
breath	years	ween		Sweden		thirty
eat		creed		English		forty
sea		deed		me		whinny
deal		meet		replied		steady

Word-study journal sample from a student at the within-word pattern stage

Long E homophones

ee	ea
see	sea
meet	meat
leech	leach-brain
tee	tea
feet	feat
beet	beat-win
bee	Bea-name
flee	flea
seem	seam
creek	creak-door
week	weak-not strong
reed	read
steel	steal-to take
heal	heal-to get better
peel	peal-bells, sounds
peek	peak-mountain
reel	real-true
leek	leak-water, oil

Word-study journal sample from a student at the within-word pattern stage

106

Long ā words

a_e			ai		ay	
Abe	came	sage	wait	grain	stay	away
rake	make	sane	sail	laid	play	Himalayan
cake	late	whale	wail	paid	tray	
take	male	crane	tail	snail	way	
name	cape	trade	rail	paint	may	
shade	tape	snake	mail	raise	say	
wade	crate	space	trail	drain	pay	
grave	create	erase	dairy	prairie	clay	
Dave	ape	maze	nail	raid	day	
crave	mate	graze	sailor	bait	bay	
shape	trace	made	rain	bail	ray	
ate	Nate	escape	again	hail	May	
sake	rate	disease	plain	chain	Kay	
wake	state	frame	pain	pail	morray	
bake	plate	fame	train	daisy	stray	
glaze	lane	amazed	stain	proclaim	lay	
shake	plane	race	complain		pray	
lace	fame	game	Maine		gay	
sake	mane	grace	vain		doorway	
face	hate	wave	strain		sway	
case	cane	save	explain		slay	
shame	dane	cave	contain		Fay	
lane	Kate	ale	main		cray	
nave	grave	tale	Spain		spray	
wages	chase	pale	strain		Kay	
scrape	date	claim			gray	
Dave	lame	stake	brain		essay	
shame	rage	stale	lain		Poway	
phase	stage	babe	trait		way	

Word-study journal sample from a student at the within-word pattern stage

Appendix F
Developmental Phases of Spelling

Grade 1	Grade 2	Grade 3	Grade 4	Grade 5	Grade 6	Grade 7	Grade 8
Alphabetic							
	Within-Word Pattern						
		Syllables and Affixes					
				Derivational Patterns			

What Students Explore at Each Developmental Phase

Alphabetic	Within-Word Pattern	Syllables and Affixes	Derivational Patterns
• Single consonants • Consonant digraphs and clusters • Short vowel patterns	• Common long vowel patterns • R- and l-influenced vowels • Common spelling for diphthongs [ou], [oi] • Compound words • Homophones • Common inflections	• Less frequent vowel patterns • Sound and meaning of common prefixes and suffixes • Common syllable patterns explained • More complex prefixes and suffixes	• Spelling-meaning connection in base words and derived parts • Greek and Latin word parts • Absorbed prefixes

Source: Houghton Mifflin

108

Appendix G
High Frequency and "No Excuses" Words

Poway Unified School District

WHAT are "high frequency words"?

High frequency words are words that are most often used in writing.

The words are listed in order from most to least common.

Many of these words are among the oldest words in our language and therefore have archaic etymologies. Since these words are the most commonly used words, we expect students to spell them correctly all the time. Therefore we are calling them "No Excuses" words. Even if a student doesn't know the spelling, he can always look it up on the class poster or list provided to keep at home.

WHERE did the words come from?

Numerous studies have identified these words.

The list of "No Excuses" words is derived from looking at word frequency in the contexts of children's writing, content-area books, and children's literature.

WHY teach high frequency words?

The 100 most frequently used words in writing comprise 50% of all words used in adult writing! Knowing these words quickly, effortlessly, and automatically gives students opportunities to think about the content of their writing rather than having to struggle over the spelling of a word. Spelling is used as a "literacy yardstick" and we want our students to "measure up" as literate communicators. An incorrectly spelled word in a written piece sends a message that the writer is illiterate or careless, and the message the writer hopes to communicate is compromised.

HOW are No Excuses (high frequency) words different from the words I teach in Houghton Mifflin?

All of the No Excuses words appear in the Houghton Mifflin program. They do not appear in order of frequency; instead, they appear whenever they happen to fit in with the linguistic element being featured. However, they are not always singled out. Since the focus of the Houghton Mifflin program is on teaching children linguistic features and patterns, there is less emphasis placed on high frequency words. In other words:

In Houghton Mifflin, words, features, and patterns can be GENERALIZED, whereas No Excuses words can be MEMORIZED!

If you think of the No Excuses words the way you think of math facts, you will have a clear understanding of how these words fit into the overall spelling competence of our students. We expect children to know these words automatically, regardless of their developmental stage. Even a very poor speller should have at least these 100 words (grade 3–8) memorized and used correctly in all of their work, all of the time!

No Excuses Words
Expectations for Grade Levels

Grade Level	Words to Be Learned from the No Excuses List
Kindergarten	Words # 1–10
First	Words # 1–50
Second	Words # 1–100
Third to Eighth	Words # 1–100

These words are found on the list of No Excuses Words on pages 112–114.

Frequently Misspelled Words

WHAT are "frequently misspelled words"?

These are words that students have been found to misspell in their daily writing.

The top three most frequently misspelled words are: *too, a lot,* and *because,* yet these words are not on the "No Excuses" list.

WHERE did the frequently misspelled lists of words come from?

Ron Cramer looked at over 18,000 samples of student writing in grades 1 through 8. Based on his exhaustive study, he developed the top 100 words that children misspell at each grade level. The list of No Excuses words is different, because it is derived from studies of word frequency in the contexts of children's writing, content-area books, and children's literature.

WHY teach frequently misspelled words?

Using lists of the top 100 misspelled words for each grade level allows us the opportunity to teach words that we know children misspell over and over again. Using Cramer's study, we can add special emphasis to the words that we know students tend to misspell most often.

HOW are frequently misspelled words different from the words I teach in Houghton Mifflin?

Up until now, our district program has only used high frequency word lists for our spelling program. With the addition of Houghton Mifflin, we are systematically teaching spelling and linguistic features and patterns in a developmental sequence. No Excuses words (high frequency words) and the Houghton Mifflin program complement one another. Cramer's research also addresses a third component not addressed by Houghton Mifflin or the No Excuses words list.

In Houghton Mifflin, words, features, and patterns are GENERALIZED, whereas "No Excuses" words are MEMORIZED! Frequently misspelled words can also be memorized!

Even very poor spellers should have at least their high frequency words memorized and used correctly in all of their work. Every student can also be expected to use the frequently misspelled words chart as a reference.

Teaching "No Excuses" and Frequently Misspelled Words

The focus is on memorization.

Word-sorting activities (or sorts) are less effective for memorizing words. Sorts are better for learning to generalize!

Teach students to MEMORIZE by using:

Flash cards
Partner checks
Dry-erase boards
Rainbow writing
Magnetic letters
Dictate-and-write exercise (timed)
Mad-minute exercise
Writing-in-the-air exercise
Ghost writing on the board
Copy, cover, write, and check

A Few Ideas for Learning No Excuses Words

1. Check spelling accuracy in all kinds of student writing, not just spelling tests. These No Excuses words in particular are ones that students very often spell correctly in isolation on a spelling test. However, in the context of other writing, they often misspell them. Check these words by counting down the first ten lines of a piece of writing for the accuracy of No Excuses words and Frequently Misspelled words.
2. Pretest students at the beginning of the year.
3. Randomly include these words on other spelling assessments.
4. Issue "spelling tickets" for spelling "violations" of the No Excuses and Frequently Misspelled words.
5. Have students "sign in" on a spelling log every time they miss one of the No Excuses or Frequently Misspelled Words. Set up the spelling log in alphabetical order with a separate page for each of the words. Have students sign in on the page of the word they missed.

"No Excuses" Words
First Grade

1. a	14. each	27. not	40. up
2. about	15. for	28. of	41. was
3. all	16. from	29. on	42. we
4. an	17. had	30. one	43. were
5. and	18. have	31. or	44. what
6. are	19. he	32. said	45. when
7. as	20. his	33. that	46. which
8. at	21. how	34. the	47. will
9. be	22. I	35. their	48. with
10. but	23. if	36. there	49. you
11. by	24. in	37. they	50. your
12. can	25. is	38. this	
13. do	26. it	39. to	

"No Excuses" Words
Second Grade

1. a	26. has	51. my	76. these
2. about	27. have	52. no	77. they
3. after	28. he	53. not	78. this
4. all	29. her	54. now	79. time
5. an	30. him	55. of	80. to
6. and	31. his	56. on	81. two
7. are	32. how	57. one	82. up
8. as	33. I	58. only	83. use
9. at	34. if	59. or	84. very
10. be	35. in	60. other	85. was
11. been	36. into	61. out	86. water
12. but	37. is	62. over	87. way
13. by	38. it	63. people	88. we
14. called	39. its	64. said	89. were
15. can	40. just	65. see	90. what
16. could	41. know	66. she	91. when
17. did	42. like	67. so	92. where
18. do	43. little	68. some	93. which
19. down	44. long	69. than	94. who
20. each	45. made	70. that	95. will
21. find	46. make	71. the	96. with
22. first	47. many	72. their	97. words
23. for	48. may	73. them	98. would
24. from	49. more	74. then	99. you
25. had	50. most	75. there	100. your

"No Excuses" Words
Third–Fifth Grade

1. a	26. has	51. my	76. these
2. about	27. have	52. no	77. they
3. after	28. he	53. not	78. this
4. all	29. her	54. now	79. time
5. an	30. him	55. of	80. to
6. and	31. his	56. on	81. two
7. are	32. how	57. one	82. up
8. as	33. I	58. only	83. use
9. at	34. if	59. or	84. very
10. be	35. in	60. other	85. was
11. been	36. into	61. out	86. water
12. but	37. is	62. over	87. way
13. by	38. it	63. people	88. we
14. called	39. its	64. said	89. were
15. can	40. just	65. see	90. what
16. could	41. know	66. she	91. when
17. did	42. like	67. so	92. where
18. do	43. little	68. some	93. which
19. down	44. long	69. than	94. who
20. each	45. made	70. that	95. will
21. find	46. make	71. the	96. with
22. first	47. many	72. their	97. words
23. for	48. may	73. them	98. would
24. from	49. more	74. then	99. you
25. had	50. most	75. there	100. your

Appendix H
Games and Activities

Effective teachers can become careful consumers of Internet resources designed to help children become better spellers. Too many students muddle through phonics activities that are too easy, too hard, or just plain not engaging enough to hold their attention. Once you learn how to create a class of "word lovers," you will approach your spelling instruction from a new perspective. You and your students will become "word scientists." Here is a list of actual and online word games that I find helpful in teaching spelling. Since it is almost impossible to stay current with URLs and contact information for companies, check my website (spellingtools. com) for updates. I am always looking for new games and resources to help teachers. If a link doesn't work or if you have trouble finding a game, just email me (cmarten@znet.com) and I will update the information on my webpage. Or, if you find new games that work well, let me know and I'll add them.

Games

Many of these games are available at your local toy store, but I have included contact information for each one in case you can't find them. Good luck and have fun!

Oh Scrud! by Martin and Associates
Phone: 435-644-5726
Email: ohscrud@xpressweb.com

This is a fast-paced spelling card game for all ages. Everyone plays at the same time (no taking turns!). For groups of 2–6 players who are wild about words!

Turbo-Twist Spelling, by Leapfrog
Phone: 1-800-701-LEAP (5327)
Website: www.leapfrog.com

In essence, a spelling test study buddy. This tool is helpful for students who need help in memorizing high frequency words and do well with auditory tasks. Students who do not have someone at home to test them on homework words would benefit from this independent study device designed for memorizing words.

Word Spin, by Geospace International
Phone: 800-800-5090
Email: contact@geospaceplay.com
Website: www.geospaceplay.com

The award-winning word game! Word Spin is a go-anywhere game fun for the whole family. It can be played by one, two, or more players or by teams. The winner of six international awards, it is simple enough for a four-year-old to learn, yet challenging enough for a college English professor! Magnetic wheels are rotated and twisted to form words. There are five variations. Even children at the letter name stage can play by looking for the letters that they know.

Webster's New World Word Madness, by Great American Puzzle Factory
Phone: 800-922-1194
Website: www.greatamericanpuzzle.com

A great game with multiple levels of play, Webster's New World Word Madness combines the fun of Go Fish! with letters. Just how creative can you be? Since this game is different each time you play it, the fun never stops. Contains 112 alphabet playing cards, score pad, and multilevel instructions. For 2–6 players. A great travel companion.

AlphaBlitz: A Word Puzzle Card Game, by Wizards of the Coast
Web site: www.wizardsofthecoast.com

Designed for 2–6 players, ages 10 and up. Fast-paced, exciting game to challenge spellers of all levels. Speed is the key. Students should be grouped by stage when playing this game in order to level the playing field. The deck of AlphaBlitz cards includes letters of the alphabet—the least common ones in red. A few cards are turned face up, and players try to come up with the longest possible word, using only the letters shown on the cards. Each letter can be used as many times as necessary, but not every card needs to be used.

Jumble Word Game, by Cadaco
Phone: 800-621-5426
Email: customerservice@cadaco.com
Website: www.cadaco.com

Unscramble the most mixed-up words in this classic family game. Two play levels, for beginner and pro. Includes 25 Jumble cards (offering 150 different Jumbles), sand timer, magic writing slate with stylus, and special Jumble score pad. For two or more players, ages 8 to adult.

Speliminate, by J & J Innovations, LLC
Phone: 414-962-7750
Email: juliet@execpc.com.

Based on the timeless travel game Ghost, this competitive word game pits player against player in a battle *not* to spell a word. Like Scrabble, Speliminate competitively tests your spelling and vocabulary knowledge. Eliminate your opponents by forcing them to complete the spelling of a word.

Scrabble, by Hasbro
Phone: 888-836-7025
Website: www.hasbro.com

A classic game that has hundreds of uses in a word-crafting classroom. Even the tiles can be used for many activities and games.

Up Words, by Hasbro
Phone: 888-836-7025
Website: www.hasbro.com

A relatively new game that turns the basic Scrabble game into a three-dimensional brain-teaser allowing words to be built down, across, diagonally, *and* up—with letters stacking on top of one another.

Online Games

Spell Check
Website: www.funbrain.com/spell/index.html
Spell Check gives students twenty sets of four words. The students have to select the incorrectly spelled word (just like on most norm-referenced standardized tests) and then they have to type it correctly. My only warning is that some of the misspelled words are rather odd misspellings. For example the word *teim* appeared in one set. I corrected it to *team* when the word they were looking for was *time*. However, if they are forewarned about this glitch, students who play this "spell check" game will learn even from these examples.

Long-Vowel Silent-E Crossword Puzzle
Website: www.surfnetkids.com/games/phonics-cw.htm

Your basic crossword puzzle with a twist, since it focuses on long vowel words using the silent *e*. This is a great site for your within-word pattern kids.

Phonics Game Show
Website: www.surfnetkids.com/quiz/phonics/

This fun site incorporates a game show theme into learning phonics generalizations. Add it to your browser's "favorites" and let your students try out a few games when they finish their work early.

Long and Short Vowel Mix & Match
Website: www.surfnetkids.com/games/phonics-mm.htm

Another site to add to your favorites as an independent word study activity. Perfect for students at the within-word pattern stage.

Long-Vowel Silent-Vowel Word Search
Website: www.surfnetkids.com/games/phonics-ws.htm

Similar to the others mentioned above. This site gives extra practice on the long vowel words that within-word pattern kids are using and confusing.

Word Search Game
Website: www.funbrain.com/detect/index.html

This great game from Funbrain.com allows students to play against the computer or to make up their own word search to print and solve on their own. I use it to help practice no-excuses words. Like all the Funbrain.com games, the students can select the level of difficulty. This site also features several premade puzzles related to books, such as *Harry Potter.*

A Feast of Homonyms
Website: www.quia.com/jg/66106.html

Four homonym games are included in this one website: matching, word search, flash cards, and concentration. Homonyms are relevant for students from the within-word pattern stage through the derivational relations stage. The layout of these games is appealing and motivating, and it also keeps track of your score!

Compound Words
Website: www.janbrett.com/piggybacks/activity

Leave it to Jan Brett to come up with a darling activity that also teaches an important concept about compound words. If you haven't seen the rest of her website, it's well worth the trip!

Internet Anagram Server
Website: www.wordsmith.org/anagram/index.html

Did you know that *parliament* is an anagram of *partial men?* Or that *Clint Eastwood* is an anagram of *Old West Action?* Someone once said, "All life's wisdom can be found in anagrams. Anagrams never lie." Here is your chance to discover the wisdom of anagrams. Enter the word or phrase of your choice in the space provided on this site, then press the button and your word turns into an anagram.

Spelling Test
Website: www.sentex.net/~mmcadams/spelling.html

Your students will enjoy taking this online spelling test to test their word knowledge. They shouldn't feel badly if they misspell a lot of these items, because most adults miss at least ten words. This site is actually better for adults. Ask your administrator to take this test and then talk about the importance of developing spelling consciousness.

WordSort Software
Website: www.hendersonedsoft.com/index.html

Although this isn't an on-line game, it's the only educational software program I have discovered that is purposefully aligned with the developmental spelling stages. You can download a free 30-day trial of this program. A free license to use a single copy is now available for educators. It is perfect for kids at the within-word pattern stage. You can start your students at any level from prephonemic through syllables and affixes. WordSort was originally conceived by the late Dr. Edmund H. Henderson, director of the University of Virginia's McGuffey Reading Center and International Reading Association Outstanding Teacher Educator in Reading in 1990. It uses the task of sorting to reveal to students the essential differences and similarities between groups of words, presenting a series of lessons in which they are asked to match words with a selection of example words.

Quiz Lab
Website: www.quizlab.com

When you go to this site you will be asked to sign up for Quiz Lab. Once you do (it's free), you have instant access to hundreds of quizzes on many subjects, including a huge section of spelling quizzes. Teachers can create their own quizzes and have students log in to the webpage to take the quiz. Instant feedback answers are also an option. Quiz results are emailed directly to the teacher. I recommend creating your own quizzes rather than using the premade ones. Their biggest problem is that most of them are multiple choice, four misspelled choices and one correct choice. When you create a spelling quiz it is better to have only one word spelled incorrectly, so that students aren't exposed to so many incorrectly spelled words.

WordCentral.com Dictionary
Website: www.wordcentral.com

Merriam-Webster's Dictionary has been a basic learning tool in our classrooms for years. This powerful and engaging website is an online version with all of the features of the paper version and more. One is a student dictionary that includes many word histories. A build-your-own-dictionary section allows students to create their own personal dictionaries. The "daily buzzword" introduces a new word every day. My students particularly enjoy the coding chamber and English experiments, located on the "second floor." Take some time just to explore all that this award-winning site has to offer.

Scripps Howard National Spelling Bee
Website: www.spellingbee.com

This site describes its purpose as helping students to "improve their spelling, increase their vocabularies, learn concepts, and develop correct English usage that will help them all their lives." I've used this site with some of my most advanced spellers who need a challenge. At the beginning of the school year there are lessons that take a student through weeks of preparation for the national spelling bee. The lessons are true word-crafting lessons that ask student to engage in all sorts of word hunting and collecting as training for the bee. Even if your students are not interested the spelling bee, these activities are great for independent study.

A.Word.A.Day
Website: www.wordsmith.org

The music and magic of words is what A.Word.A.Day (AWAD) is all about. This website sends a vocabulary word and its definition to subscribers every day. Currently, AWAD is subscribed to by over 384,000 linguaphiles, in more than 195 countries. Subscription is free, and interesting facts about words will arrive in your email every day. The most useful part of this daily email for me has been that the words are based on a weekly theme. For example, one week all the definitions were for "coined" words. These themes lead to very intriguing word-study discussions with students who are in the derivational relations stage!

Letter-by-Letter Word Games
Website: www.gtoal.com/wordgames/games.html

This website appears to be designed for "word game programmers," but I found it of interest. The website creators, Graham Toal and Steffan O'Sullivan, list over 450 published word games, all of them letter-by-letter, or *word-building*, games (to distinguish them from word games that use whole words, phrases, sentences, and so on, like Taboo, Guesstures, Trivial Pursuit, and charades, all of which may be considered "word games" but are outside the scope of this list). Toal and O'Sullivan are collectors of these games and provide excellent reviews and descriptions. While many of these games are collector's editions or foreign language versions, it is nevertheless an exhaustive list.

Appendix I
Effective Spelling Instruction

**Professional References | Children's Literature | Assessments
High Frequency Words | Word-Study Links**

Effective spelling teachers are equipped with tools to help students become expert spellers and develop a love of words and language.

In order to be an effective word-study teacher you will need many tools in your tool cabinet. Gone are the days when teaching spelling simply required one tool: a drill. Now we know that memorizing is not enough. Herein lies the power of word study. The best place to begin is with assessments to help you clearly identify each student's developmental stage of spelling. There are many tools you can use to determine a child's spelling stage. One of the more systematic and common tools is a developmental spelling inventory like those published in *Words Their Way* and *Word Journeys*. Here are the assessments I have adapted from *Words Their Way*. We use these in our district for grades K–8. These tools serve as a way to MEASURE developmental progress and inform instructional decisions.

Spelling Inventories

Depending on which author or study you read there are different names for each developmental stage, but the characteristics of each stage are the same. Click on any of the sections below to learn about each stage. For each stage you will find: descriptions of the stage, linguistic features to be learned, samples of student writing at that stage, websites to support students at that stage, additional word lists for that stage.

Letter Name Stage   Within-Word Pattern Stage
Syllables and Affixes Stage   Derivational Relations Stage

Your tool chest would not be complete if you didn't have a fully stocked bookshelf of resources to support your technical knowledge and help you develop your expertise, skills, and knowledge about words, spelling, and word study.

Professional References

This link will give you a list of all the professional books that I have found helpful to an understanding of effective word study.

Children's Literature

Click on this link for an annotated list of children's books that spark an interest in words. Each title links directly to amazon.com so you can purchase the book.

Word-Study Links

Here you will find a collection of links to websites and online resources to help supplement your spelling instruction.

Appendix J
Phonetic Spelling Inventory

WHAT?

The Phonetic Spelling Inventory is a short spelling assessment to help the teacher learn about each student's orthographic knowledge. The results of the spelling inventory will have implications for reading, writing, vocabulary, and spelling instruction.

This assessment measures the student's:

- Application of knowledge of the alphabetic principle in writing words.
- Application of specific features in spelling words.
- Utilization of conventional spelling in writing words.
- Stage/substage of spelling.

WHY?

The English language is based on the alphabetic code. In order to be an effective reader and writer, the student needs to understand how to use this code. Spelling is a window into the student's knowledge of how the alphabet works. The way in which students apply this knowledge can be seen in the way they spell words, whether in an inventive fashion or conventionally. By administering the Phonetic Spelling Inventory, the teacher can determine the stage of spelling development for each student. This provides the teacher with information that can guide the formation of flexible groups and drive appropriate instruction.

WHO?

This assessment is appropriate for students who demonstrate a basic knowledge of the alphabet code as evidenced in writing.

HOW?

Administration

The beginning section of the Phonetic Word Lists should be administered to the whole class. The remainder can be given to small groups of students who are able to continue. Let the students know that this inventory is not a test, but that it will help the teacher learn about how they spell.

The teacher needs to look at the students' papers after administering the beginning section to the whole class to determine which students need to continue. Teacher judgment is necessary. The assessment recommends that the previous assessment level be given to students who miss five out of the first eight words.

Scoring and Analysis

The analysis begins with determining how many words were spelled correctly. Count the errors and report the ratio of correct to total. The student's spelling stage usually corresponds to the number of words written correctly.

However, more qualitative information than the number of errors is needed to determine a stage of spelling development or to plan appropriate activities to meet student needs. Here's where the Feature Guide comes in. Because each form highlights a progression (each stage is further divided into substages of *early*, **middle**, and **late**), it will be apparent when a student's knowledge fades or gives out, as well as what features students have mastered and which ones they are still working to master. With the help of the information on the Feature Guide, a teacher, at a glance, should be able to form groups based on the information recorded.

Phonetic Spelling Inventory—Student Response Form

Date _____

Level _____

Total Score

Student: _____

1. _____
2. _____
3. _____
4. _____
5. _____

6. _____
7. _____
8. _____
9. _____
10. _____

11. _____
12. _____
13. _____
14. _____
15. _____

16. _____
17. _____
18. _____
19. _____
20. _____

21. _____
22. _____
23. _____
24. _____
25. _____

Phonetic Spelling Inventory—Student Response Form

NAME: _____

DATE: _____

Circle Inventory Level Used: I   II   III   IV

Percent Correct: _____%

Circle Stage: LN   WWP   SA   DR

1. _____
2. _____
3. _____
4. _____
5. _____
6. _____
7. _____
8. _____
9. _____
10. _____
11. _____
12. _____
13. _____
14. _____
15. _____
16. _____
17. _____
18. _____
19. _____
20. _____
21. _____
22. _____
23. _____
24. _____
25. _____

Phonetic Spelling Inventory—Student Response Form

NAME: _____

DATE: _____

Circle Inventory Level Used: I   II   III   IV

Percent Correct: _____%

Circle Stage: LN   WWP   SA   DR

1. _____
2. _____
3. _____
4. _____
5. _____
6. _____
7. _____
8. _____
9. _____
10. _____
11. _____
12. _____
13. _____
14. _____
15. _____
16. _____
17. _____
18. _____
19. _____
20. _____
21. _____
22. _____
23. _____
24. _____
25. _____

Phonetic Spelling Inventory Word List—Level I

Instructions: Let the students know that you are administering this inventory to learn about how they spell. Let them know that this is not a test, but that they will be helping you be a better teacher by doing their best. **Students are not to study these words.** The results will be invalid if students have been formally taught or exposed to these words.

Call the words as you would for any test. Use the words in a sentence to be sure the students know the exact word.

Possible script: "I am going to ask you to spell some words. Try to spell them the best you can. Some of the words will be easy to spell; some will be more difficult. When you do not know how to spell a word, spell it the best you can."

Have students check their papers for their names and the date.

Set One

1. fan   I am a baseball fan. *fan*
2. pet   I have a pet cat. *pet*
3. dig   He will dig a hole. *dig*
4. mop   He said he will use a mop to clean up the mess. *mop*
5. rope   The rope was used to tie the box to the top of the car. *rope*

Set Two

6. wait   You will need to wait for a letter. *wait*
7. chunk   A chunk of ice fell off the roof. *chunk*
8. sled   The dog sled was pulled by huskies. *sled*
9. stick   I used a stick to poke in the hole. *stick*
10. shine   He rubbed the coin to make it shine. *shine*

Set Three

11. dream   Do you ever dream of being an astronaut? *dream*
12. blade   He bought a new blade for his skates. *blade*
13. coach   The coach called the team over to the bench. *coach*
14. fright   She was a fright in her Halloween costume. *fright*
15. snowing   It would be snowing if it were a little colder. *snowing*

Set Four

16. talked   They talked all day about their trip. *talked*
17. camping   Shirley said that her family went camping. *camping*
18. thorn   The thorn from the rose bush stuck in his finger. *thorn*
19. shouted   They shouted at the driver as he ran through a red light. *shouted*
20. spoil   The food will spoil if it sits out too long. *spoil*

Set Five

21. grow   The plant will grow six inches in the summer. *grow*
22. chirp   The baby birds will chirp when they are hungry. *chirp*
23. clapped   The magician clapped her hands twice and the alligator vanished. *clapped*
24. tries   In basketball, the center tries to block the shot. *tries*
25. hiking   They started hiking up the mountain this morning. *hiking*

Phonetic Spelling Inventory Feature Guide—Level I

Student _____ Teacher _____ Grade _____ Date _____ Total Points ___/60

Percent of Words Correct _____ %

Stages	Emergent late		Letter Name–Alphabetic			Within-Word Pattern		Syllables & Affixes	Points
	Consonant		early	middle	late	early	middle / late	early / middle / late	
Features	Initial	Final	Short Vowels	Digraphs	Blends	Long Vowel Patterns	Vowel Team/ Diphthong and R-Control Vowels	Syllable Junctures, Consonant Doubling, Inflected Endings, Prefixes, Suffixes	
Possible Points	6	6	7	8	13	6	6	8	
1. fan	f		a						
2. pet	p	t	e						
3. dig	d	g	i						
4. mop	m	p	o						
5. rope	r	p				o-e			
6. wait	w	t				ai			
7. chunk			u	ch	nk				
8. sled			e		sl				
9. stick			i	ck	st				
10. shine				sh		i-e			
11. dream					dr	ea			
12. blade					bl	a-e			
13. coach				-ch		oa			
14. fright				-ght	fr				
15. snowing					sn		ow	-ing	
16. talked					lk			-ed	
17. camping					-mp			-ing	
18. thorn				th			or		
19. shouted				sh			ou	-ed	
20. spoil					sp		oi		
21. grow					gr		ow		
22. chirp				ch			ir		
23. clapped					cl			pp -ed	
24. tries					tr			-ies	
25. hiking								-ing	
Totals	/6	/6	/7	/8	/13	/6	/6	/8	/60

Classroom Composite for Phonetic Spelling Inventory Feature Guide—Level I

Teacher _____

Grade _____

Date _____

Student Names	Total Points	Consonants Initial	Final	Short Vowels	Digraphs	Blends	Long Vowel Patterns	Vowel Team/ Diphthong and R-Control Vowels	Syllable Junctures, Consonant Doubling, Inflected Endings, Prefixes, Suffixes
Stages		Emergent late		Letter Name–Alphabetic early	middle	late	Within-Word Pattern early	middle late	Syllables & Affixes early middle late
Features / % Correct									
Possible Points →	60	6	6	7	8	13	6	6	8
1.									
2.									
3.									
4.									
5.									
6.									
7.									
8.									
9.									
10.									
11.									
12.									
13.									
14.									
15.									
16.									
17.									
18.									
19.									
20.									
21.									
22.									
23.									
24.									
25.									
Number who missed two or more									
Average									

Phonetic Spelling Inventory Word List–Level II

This is a short spelling inventory to help you learn about your students' orthographic knowledge. The results of the spelling inventories will have implications for reading, writing, vocabulary, and spelling instruction. **Students are not to study these words.** The results will be invalid if students have been formally taught or exposed to these words.

Instructions: Let the students know that you are administering this inventory to learn about how they spell. Let them know that this is not a test, but that they will be helping you be a better teacher by doing their best.

Possible script: "I am going to ask you to spell some words. Try to spell them the best you can. Some of the words will be easy to spell; some will be more difficult. When you do not know how to spell a word, spell it the best you can."

Have students check their papers for their names and the date.

Set One

1. bed — I hopped out of bed this morning. *bed*
2. ship — The ship sailed around the island. *ship*
3. when — When will you come back? *when*
4. lump — He had a lump on his head after he fell. *lump*
5. float — I can float on the water with my new raft. *float*

Set Two

6. train — I rode the train to the next town. *train*
7. place — I found a new place to put my books. *place*
8. drive — I learned to drive a car. *drive*
9. bright — The light is very bright. *bright*
10. shopping — Mother went shopping at the grocery store. *shopping*

Set Three

11. spoil — The food will spoil if it is not kept cool. *spoil*
12. serving — The restaurant is serving dinner tonight. *serving*
13. chewed — The dog chewed up my favorite sweater yesterday. *chewed*
14. carries — She carries apples in her basket. *carries*
15. marched — We marched in the parade. *marched*

Set Four

16. shower — The shower in the bathroom was very hot. *shower*
17. cattle — The cowboy rounded up the cattle. *cattle*
18. favor — He did his brother a favor by taking out the trash. *favor*
19. ripen — The fruit will ripen over the next few days. *ripen*
20. cellar — I went down to the cellar for the can of paint. *cellar*

Set Five

21. pleasure — It was a pleasure to listen to the choir sing. *pleasure*
22. fortunate — It was fortunate that the driver had snow tires during the snowstorm. *fortunate*
23. confident — I am confident that we can win the game. *confident*
26. civilize — They had the idea that they could civilize the forest people. *civilize*
26. opposition — The coach said the opposition would give us a tough game. *opposition*

Phonetic Spelling Inventory Feature Guide—Level II

Student _____ Teacher _____ Grade _____ Date _____

Total Points /66
Words Spelled Correctly /25
Percent Correct ____ %

Stages	Emergent	Letter Name–Alphabetic				Within-Word Pattern		Syllables & Affixes	Derivational Relations		Total Points
		Consonants									
Features		Initial	Final	Short Vowels	Digraphs & Blends	Long Vowel Patterns	Other Vowel Patterns	Syllable Junctures, Consonant Doubling, Inflected Endings, Prefixes, Suffixes	Bases & Roots	Word	
		early		middle	late	early middle late	late	early middle late			
Possible Points →	2		6	5	13	5	6	24	5	Word	66
1. bed	b	d								bed	66
2. ship		p		i	sh					ship	
3. when		n		e	wh					when	
4. lump	l			u	mp					lump	
5. float		t			fl	oa				float	
6. train		n			tr	ai				train	
7. place					pl	a-e				place	
8. drive		v			dr	i-e				drive	
9. bright					br	igh				bright	
10. shopping				o	sh			pp	ing		shopping	
11. spoil					sp		oi			spoil	
12. serving							er	ing		serving	
13. chewed					ch		ew	ed		chewed	
14. carries								rr	ies		carries	
15. marched					ch		ar	ed		marched	
16. shower					sh		ow	er		shower	
17. cattle								tt	le		cattle	
18. favor								av	or		favor	
19. ripen								ip	en		ripen	
20. cellar								ll	ar		cellar	
21. pleasure								ure	pleas	pleasure	
22. fortunate							or	ate	fortun	fortunate	
23. confident								con	ent	fid	confident	
24. civilize								ize	civil	civilize	
25. opposition								op pp tion	pos	opposition	
Totals	/2	/6	/5	/13	/5	/6	/24	/5		/66

Phonetic Spelling Inventory Error Guide—Level II

Directions: Circle student's spelling attempts below. If a spelling is not listed, write it in where it belongs on the developmental continuum. Circle the spelling stage that summarizes the student's development.

Student _____ Teacher _____ Grade _____ Date _____

Number spelled correctly/ Number of words attempted _____ / _____

Features	Emergent — Consonants (Initial Final): middle, late	Letter Name–Alphabetic — Short Vowels: early, middle, late	Digraphs & Blends: early, middle, late	Within-Word Pattern — Long Vowel Patterns: early, middle, late	Other Vowel Patterns: early, middle, late	Syllable Junctures, Consonant Doubling, Inflected Endings, Prefixes, Suffixes — Syllables & Affixes: early, middle, late	Bases & Roots — Derivational Relations: early
1. bed	b · bd	bad · bed · <u>bed</u>					
2. ship	s · sp shp	sep	shep · <u>ship</u>				
3. when	w · yn wn	wan	whan · <u>when</u>				
4. lump	l · lp lmp	lop	lomp · <u>lump</u>				
5. float	f · ft vt flt	fot · flot · flott		flowt · flaout flote · <u>float</u>			
6. train	j · t trn	jran · chran tan tran		teran · traen trane · <u>train</u>			
7. place	p · ps pls	pas · palac plas plac		pase · plais plase · <u>place</u>			
8. drive	d · j jrv drf	drv griv jriv driv		jrive · drieve draive · <u>drive</u>			
9. bright	b · bt brt	bit · brit		bite · brite briete · <u>bright</u>			
10. shopping	s sp · spg shp	sapg	sopn shapng shopn shopen		sopin shopin shoping	shopping · <u>shopping</u>	
11. spoil					spol sole sool · spoyle spole spoal · <u>spoil</u>		
12. serving						sefng srvng sering · serfng surving serveing · <u>serving</u>	
13. chewed					cud cooed cued coyed chued chood · cuwed chud chowd choud chewd · <u>chewed</u>		
14. carries						keres cares carres carise carys cairries carrys · <u>carries</u>	
15. marched						much march marchd marcht marched · <u>marched</u>	
16. shower					shewr shuor shawer shuor shower · <u>shower</u>		
17. cattle					catl cadol	catel catle cattel · <u>cattle</u>	
18. favor						favr faver favir · <u>favor</u>	
19. ripen						ribn ripn ripun ripan ripon · <u>ripen</u>	
20. cellar						salr selr celr · salar seler · seller celler · <u>cellar</u>	
21. pleasure						plasr plager plejer pleser plesher plesour plesure	<u>pleasure</u>
22. fortunate						forhnat frehnit foohinit forchenut fochininte fortunet	<u>fortunate</u>
23. confident						confadent confedint confedent confadent · confadent confednet confednt confodent	<u>confident</u>
24. civilize						sivils sevelies sivilice cifillazas sivelize · sivalize civalise civilise	<u>civilize</u>
25. opposition						opasion opasishan opozcison opishien oposition · oppasishion opasitian opasition oposision	<u>opposition</u>

131

Classroom Composite for Phonetic Spelling Inventory Feature Guide—Level II

Teacher _____ Grade _____ Date _____

Stages → Features		Emergent late	Letter Name–Alphabetic early middle late		Within-Word Pattern early middle late		Syllables & Affixes early middle late	Derivational Relations
Student Names	% Correct / Total Points	Consonants Initial / Final	Short Vowels	Digraphs & Blends	Long Vowel Patterns	Other Vowel Patterns	Syllable Junctures, Consonant Doubling, Inflected Endings, Prefixes, Suffixes	Bases & Roots
Possible Points → 66		2 / 6	5	13	5	6	24	5
1.								
2.								
3.								
4.								
5.								
6.								
7.								
8.								
9.								
10.								
11.								
12.								
13.								
14.								
15.								
16.								
17.								
18.								
19.								
20.								
21.								
22.								
23.								
24.								
25.								
Number who missed two or more								
Average %								

Phonetic Spelling Inventory Word List—Level III

This is a short spelling inventory to help you learn about your students' orthographic knowledge. The results of the spelling inventories will have implications for reading, writing, vocabulary, and spelling instruction. **Students are not to study these words.** The results will be invalid if students have been formally taught or exposed to these words.

Instructions: Let the students know that you are administering this inventory to learn about how they spell. Let them know that this is not a test, but that they will be helping you be a better teacher by doing their best.

Possible script: "I am going to ask you to spell some words. Try to spell them the best you can. Some of the words will be easy to spell; some will be more difficult. When you do not know how to spell a word, spell it the best you can."

Have students check their papers for their names and the date.

Set One

1. speck — There was a speck of mud on his windshield. *speck*
2. switch — The light switch was turned on. *switch*
3. throat — The doctor said the baby had a sore throat. *throat*
4. nurse — The nurse told the patient that her fever was high. *nurse*
5. scrape — The carpenter will scrape the paint off of the desk. *scrape*

Set Two

6. charge — What will you charge for this coat? *charge*
7. phone — Please use the phone to call home. *phone*
8. smudge — You could see the smudge of chocolate on the paper. *smudge*
9. point — The point of the knife was sharp. *point*
10. squirt — The clown had a flower to squirt water. *squirt*

Set Three

11. drawing — The drawing of the horse was done in charcoal. *drawing*
12. trapped — The miners were trapped in the tunnel for two days. *trapped*
13. waving — The crowd was waving to the senator as the train left the station. *waving*
14. powerful — The jaws were powerful for chewing food. *powerful*
15. battle — They won the battle but lost the war. *battle*

Set Four

16. fever — A high fever can be dangerous. *fever*
17. lesson — The music lesson was last Tuesday. *lesson*
18. pennies — They danced for pennies at the fair. *pennies*
19. fraction — One-half is a fraction. *fraction*
20. sailor — To be a sailor on the high seas was his dream. *sailor*

Set Five

21. distance — What is the distance from here to there? *distance*
22. confusion — There was some confusion about who would drive to the movie. *confusion*
23. discovery — The scientist made a discovery after many hours in the lab. *discovery*
26. resident — How long have you been a resident of this state? *resident*
26. visible — The star was visible with a telescope. *visible*

Phonetic Spelling Inventory Feature Guide—Level III

Student _____ Teacher _____ Grade _____ Date _____

Total Points _____ /58   Words Spelled Correctly _____ /25   **Percent Correct** _____ %

Features	Short Vowels	Digraphs & Blends (middle)	Digraphs & Blends (late)	Long Vowel Patterns	Other Vowel Patterns, Complex Consonants (middle)	Other Vowel Patterns, Complex Consonants (late)	Syllable Junctures, Consonant Doubling, Inflected Endings, Prefixes, Suffixes (early)	Syllable Junctures, Consonant Doubling, Inflected Endings, Prefixes, Suffixes (late)	Bases & Roots	Word	Total Points
Possible Points	6	8		4	11		23		6		58
1. speck	e	sp	ck							speck	
2. switch	i	sw				tch				switch	
3. throat				o-a		thr				throat	
4. nurse					ur					nurse	
5. scrape				a-e		scr				scrape	
6. charge		ch			ar					charge	
7. phone		ph		o-e						phone	
8. smudge	u	sm				dge				smudge	
9. point			nt		oi					point	
10. squirt					ir	squ				squirt	
11. drawing		dr			aw			ing		drawing	
12. trapped	a						pp	ed		trapped	
13. waving								ing		waving	
14. powerful					ow		er	ful		powerful	
15. battle	a						tt	le		battle	
16. fever							ev	er		fever	
17. lesson							ss	on		lesson	
18. pennies	e						nn	ies		pennies	
19. fraction								tion	frac	fraction	
20. sailor				ai				or		sailor	
21. distance								ance	dis	distance	
22. confusion							con	sion	fus	confusion	
23. discovery							dis	ery	cov	discovery	
24. resident								ent	resid	resident	
25. visible								ible	vis	visible	
Totals	/6	/8		/4	/11		/23		/6		/58

Classroom Composite for Phonetic Spelling Inventory Feature Guide—Level III

Teacher _____

Grade _____

Date _____

Student Names	% Correct	Total Points	Stages / Features	Letter Name–Alphabetic: early middle Short Vowels	Letter Name–Alphabetic: late Digraphs & Blends	Within-Word Pattern: early Long Vowel Patterns	Within-Word Pattern: middle late Other Vowel Patterns and tch, dge	Syllables & Affixes: early middle late Syllable Junctures, Consonant Doubling, Inflected Endings, Prefixes, Suffixes	Derivational Relations: Bases & Roots
Possible Points →		58		6	8	4	11	23	6
1.									
2.									
3.									
4.									
5.									
6.									
7.									
8.									
9.									
10.									
11.									
12.									
13.									
14.									
15.									
16.									
17.									
18.									
19.									
20.									
21.									
22.									
23.									
24.									
25.									
Number who missed two or more									
Average									

Phonetic Spelling Inventory Word List—Level IV

This is a short spelling inventory to help you learn about your students' orthographic knowledge. The results of the spelling inventories will have implications for reading, writing, vocabulary, and spelling instruction. **Students are not to study these words.** The results will be invalid if students have been formally taught or exposed to these words.

Instructions: Let the students know that you are administering this inventory to learn about how they spell. Let them know that this is not a test, but that they will be helping you be a better teacher by doing their best.

Possible script: "I am going to ask you to spell some words. Try to spell them the best you can. Some of the words will be easy to spell; some will be more difficult. When you do not know how to spell a word, spell it the best you can."

Have students check their papers for their names and the date.

1. confusion — There was confusion when there was a power failure. *confusion*
2. pleasure — It was our pleasure to have you come over. *pleasure*
3. resident — Mr. Squires has been a resident of this town for over forty years. *resident*
4. confidence — I have confidence in Donna. *confidence*
5. fortunate — We were fortunate to have gotten back safely. *fortunate*
6. opposition — The coach said the opposition would give us a tough game. *opposition*
7. prosperity — During this period of prosperity, our income increased dramatically. *prosperity*
8. succession — He fired several shots in rapid succession. *succession*

If you wish, stop here, check papers, discontinue, or go to Spelling Inventory—
Level III if a student misspells five out of the first eight words.

9. emphasize — In conclusion, I want to emphasize the most important points. *emphasize*
10. correspond — The president must correspond with many people each day. *correspond*
11. commotion — The audience heard the commotion backstage. *commotion*
12. propellant — The booster rocket is fueled by a liquid propellant. *propellant*
13. hilarious — John thought the comedian was absolutely hilarious. *hilarious*
14. criticize — The boss will criticize you for your work. *criticize*
15. reversible — Terry wears a reversible coat in the winter. *reversible*
16. category — I will put the bottles in one category and the cans in another. *category*
17. adjourn — The meeting will adjourn at five o'clock. *adjourn*
18. excerpt — I am going to read one excerpt from this chapter. *excerpt*
21. indictment — The attorney general made the indictment based on the grand jury's findings. *indictment*
21. camouflage — The soldier wore camouflage to avoid detection. *camouflage*

Phonetic Spelling Inventory Feature Guide—Level IV

Student _____ Teacher _____ Grade _____ Date _____

Total Points _____ /66
Words Spelled Correctly _____ /25
Percent Correct _____ %

Stages	Syllables & Affixes			Derivational Relations			
	early	middle	late		early		
Features	Consonant Doubling	Prefixes	Suffixes & Endings	Vowels in the Middle	Bases & Roots	Word	Total Points
Possible Points →	4	15	16	5	20		60
1. confusion		con-	-sion		fus	confusion	
2. pleasure			-ure		pleas	pleasure	
3. resident			-ent		resid	resident	
4. confidence		con-	-ence		fid	confidence	
5. fortunate			-ate		fortun	fortunate	
6. opposition	pp	op	-tion	i	pos	opposition	
7. prosperity		pro	-ity	i	sper	prosperity	
8. succession		suc	-sion		cess	succession	
9. emphasize		em	-ize		phas	emphasize	
10. correspond	rr	cor			spond	correspond	
11. commotion	mm	com	-tion	o	mot	commotion	
12. propellant	ll	pro	ant		pel	propellant	
13. hilarious			-ious		hilar	hilarious	
14. criticize			-cize	i	crit	criticize	
15. reversible		re	-ible		vers	reversible	
16. category		cat		e	egory	category	
17. adjourn		ad			journ	adjourn	
18. excerpt		ex			cerpt	excerpt	
19. indictment		in	-ment		dict	indictment	
20. camouflage		cam	-age		moufl	camouflage	
Totals	/4	/15	/16	/5	/20		/20

Phonetic Spelling Inventory Error Guide—Level IV

Student _____ Teacher _____ Grade _____ Date _____

Number spelled correctly/ _____ / _____
Number of words attempted

Features → Spelling Stages ↓	Long Vowel Patterns, Other Vowel Patterns — Within-Word Pattern		Syllable Junctures, Consonant Doubling, Inflected Endings, Prefixes, Suffixes — Syllables and Affixes			Bases and Roots — Derivational Relations		
	middle	late	early	middle	late	early	middle	late
1. confusion	confushion	confution	confustion	confulsion confusion	confusetion confussion			<u>confusion</u>
2. pleasure		plasr plager plejer	pleser	plesher	plesour pleasur pleasur			<u>pleasure</u>
3. resident	resatin	reserdent	resadent	resedent	reseadent resedent residant	resedant		<u>resident</u>
4. confidence			confadents	confadence	confedense confidence confidense	confidence confidense		<u>confidence</u>
5. fortunate		fortinat frehnit foohinit		forchenut fochininte	fortunet			<u>fortunate</u>
6. opposition		opasion	opasishan opozcison	opasitian	opasition oposision oposition	oposishan oposition oposiraty	prosperaty	<u>opposition</u>
7. prosperity	propaty propary		property	prosperaty	prosparity prosperaty prosperaty	prosperaty		<u>prosperity</u>
8. succession	sucksession		sucession	sucession	sucession succession succession	succession succesion successtion		<u>succession</u>
9. emphasize	infaside infacize		ephacize	empasize	emfsize	emfsize imfasize emphisize	emphisize	<u>emphasize</u>
10. correspond		corspond	corispond	corspond	corespond	corrospond		<u>correspond</u>
11. commotion		cmoushown comoshion	comosion	camotion comotion	cumotion comocian comossion comotion			<u>commotion</u>
12. propellant	porpelent	porpelont	proplent propelont	porpelontt propelent	propelant proppellent proppellentt	propellant		<u>propellant</u>
13. hilarious	halaris halerace halaryous		hollarries	halaries hollarous	hallarious hulariese helariuse	hularius hilerious helarious	helarious	<u>hilarious</u>
14. criticize	critise crisize	critize	crisize critise	critisise critizize critisize critisise	critasize critisise	criticise		<u>criticize</u>
15. reversible	reversbell	reversabul	reversobol	reversabel	reverseable reversabile	revercible reversable	reversable	<u>reversible</u>
16. category	cadagoure		kadacorey cadacory	catagery catigory catorgory catigorie category	cadigore catagore	catagore		<u>category</u>
17. adjourn		ajurn agern	ajurn ajorne	ajourn ajurne	agurn adjorn adjurn	adjurn adjourne		<u>adjourn</u>
18. excerpt	exherpt exhert	exherpt	exsort exserpt	exerpt ecsert	exsert excert excert	exsurpt exserpt	excerpt	<u>excerpt</u>
19. indictment		enditment inditment	enditment	iditment iditement	inditement endightment	indightment indicment	indictment	<u>indictment</u>
20. camouflage	camaflag	camoflosh comoflodge	camaphlauge	camaflage camaflage	camaflage camofloge	camaflooge	camoflage camoflouge	<u>camouflage</u>

Classroom Composite for Phonetic Spelling Inventory Feature Guide—Level IV

Teacher _____

Grade _____

Date _____

Student Names	% Correct	Total Points	Stage / Feature	Syllables & Affixes early — Consonant Doubling	Syllables & Affixes middle — Prefixes	Syllables & Affixes late — Suffixes & Endings	Derivational Relations — Vowels in the Middle	Derivational Relations — Bases & Roots
Possible Points →		60		4	15	16	5	20
1.								
2.								
3.								
4.								
5.								
6.								
7.								
8.								
9.								
10.								
11.								
12.								
13.								
14.								
15.								
16.								
17.								
18.								
19.								
20.								
21.								
22.								
23.								
24.								
25.								
Number who missed two or more								
Average								

Appendix K
Ideas for Parents and Caregivers

Beginning (Prephonemic, Early Letter Name)

1. Stay seated after a movie is over and watch the credits roll. Have your child find all the letters in his or her name, or look for all of the *C*s.
2. Go through a magazine with your child, looking for pictures of things that begin with a certain letter. Connect it to something meaningful. If your child's name begins with a *B*, look for pictures of things that start with *B*. Make a page that has a big *B* on the top. Have your child cut out all the pictures of things that start with *B* and paste them onto the page.
3. Encourage writing at home by having a "writing table" that is stocked with:
   - Many kinds of writing instruments: pencils, pens, crayons, markers.
   - Many kinds of paper: cards, envelopes, construction paper, different-colored paper, lined paper, plain paper, graph paper.
   - Scissors.
   - Glue.
   - Tape.
4. Write letters to your child. You can put little notes to her on her writing table or in her lunchbox. You might also want to encourage her to write back to you.
5. When you are preparing to go to the grocery store, invite your child to help you with the shopping list. If your child needs more apple juice for his lunch box, have him look at the word *apple juice* on the box and tell you how to spell the word. He will read the letters to you as you write them on the list. When you are at the store, in the juice section, have your child find the apple juice and match the wording on the label to your list.
6. Cut out letters from magazines so your child can see all the different ways a letter can look.

Developing (Late Letter Name, Within-Word Pattern)

When students are at this stage of development, they are becoming aware of their spelling errors and they often want to spell everything "the right way."

1. If the word your child is attempting is one of her "accountability" words, have her first try to write the word three different ways, circle the one that "looks right," and then check the word on her portable word wall. This activity will accomplish three spelling goals: raising spelling consciousness, developing the use of references, and building a stronger visual memory.
2. If the word your child is attempting is a new word, have him write it down. Possible language: "Use all that you know about letters, sounds, and patterns, and work out the best spelling you can of the word." After the first attempt, have him write the word two other ways—his "best attempts." Then have him look at the three attempts and circle the one that looks right. After going through this process, students often come up with the correct spelling.

3. Play spelling games using common patterns. For example, if your child is practicing the common pattern *ai*, you can make up letter cards that contain common beginnings (*b, c, d, m, p, sh, str, pl, dr*, etc.) and cards that contain common endings (*t, nt, l, m, st, n, r*, etc.) Have your child match up the cards before and after the common *ai* vowel combination to make up new words.

Secure (Syllable Juncture, Derivational Constancy)

1. Explore common suffixes and prefixes. Have your child begin a collection of words that start with any of the following prefixes:

anti
auto
bi
circum
co
de
en
em
ex
micro
mis
pre
sub
tele
trans

2. Also collect words with common suffixes:

age
ary
ceed
er
ful
ion
ish
ist
ive
ize
less
ment
ness
ship
th
y

3. Challenge your child in word games such as Scrabble and Boggle. Be sure to have a good dictionary nearby.

4. If you have online access, there are many excellent resources that have to do with words and spelling. Here are two excellent websites for spelling at this stage:

http://www.spellingbee.com/cctoc.shtml
This site has exciting activities that change weekly. (All previous lessons are also available.) It is a required site for any student who participates in the National Spelling Bee competition. Even if your child isn't participating, the site has excellent resources and high-level activities, as well as discussions about word explorations.

http://www.m-w.com/netdict.htm
This is the *Merriam Webster's Dictionary* site; it has links to many word study activities, including vocabulary challenges, and it's a perfect tool for looking up spelling and definitions online.

Appendix L
English Is a Difficult Language!

I don't recommend using these poems with students until they are at least at the later stages of development. They will not make sense or be funny to a student who is only at the letter name stage.

The Chaos
Dearest creature in creation,
Study English pronunciation.
I will teach you in my verse
Sounds like corpse, corps, horse, and worse.
I will keep you, Suzy, busy,
Make your head with heat grow dizzy.
Tear in eye, your dress will tear.
So shall I! Oh hear my prayer.

Just compare heart, beard, and heard,
Dies and diet, lord and word,
Sword and sward, retain and Britain.
(Mind the latter, how it's written.)
Now I surely will not plague you
With such words as plaque and ague.
But be careful how you speak:
Say break and steak, but bleak and streak;
Cloven, oven, how and low,
Script, receipt, show, poem, and toe.

Billet does not rhyme with ballet,
Bouquet, wallet, mallet, chalet.
Blood and flood are not like food,
Nor is mould like should and would.

Doll and roll and some and home.
Stranger does not rhyme with anger.

Finally, which rhymes with enough—
Though, through, plough, or dough, or cough?
Hiccough has the sound of cup.
My advice is to give up!!!

Here's a poem to use in word study with advanced students who are examining plurals.

We'll begin with a box and the plural is boxes.
But the plural of ox should be oxen, not oxes.
The one fowl is a goose but two are called geese,
Yet the plural of mouse should never be meese.
You may find a lone mouse or a whole set of mice,
Yet the plural of house is houses not hice.

If the plural of man is always called men,
Why shouldn't the plural of pan be called pen?
If I speak of a foot and you show me your feet,
And I give you a boot, would a pair be called beet?
If one is a tooth and a whole set are teeth,
Why should not the plural of booth be called beeth?

We speak of a brother and also of brethren,
But though we say Mother, we never say Methren,
Then the masculine pronouns are he, his and him,
But imagine the feminine she, shis and shim.
So English, I fancy you will all agree,
Is the funniest language you ever did see.

Funny Words
English has some funny words
They give my mind the jitters
They sound the same to you and me,
But are spelled with different letters.
There's see and sea
And be and bee
It's terribly confusing!
There's new and knew
And through and threw.
It's really not amusing!
There's deer and dear
And here and hear.
It's horribly disturbing!
There's there and their
And bare and bear.
It's really most perturbing!

Reasons Why the English Language Is Hard to Learn

The bandage was wound around the wound.

The farm was used to produce produce.

The dump was so full that it had to refuse more refuse.

We must polish the Polish furniture.

He could lead if he would get the lead out.

The soldier decided to desert his dessert in the desert.

Since there is no time like the present, he thought it was time to present the present.

A bass was painted on the head of the bass drum.

When shot at, the dove dove into the bushes.

I did not object to the object.

The insurance was invalid for the invalid.

There was a row among the oarsmen about how to row.

They were too close to the door to close it.

The buck does funny things when the does are present.

A seamstress and a sewer fell down into a sewer line.

To help with planting, the farmer taught his sow to sow.

The wind was too strong to wind the sail.

After a number of injections my jaw got number.

Upon seeing the tear in the painting I shed a tear.

I had to subject the subject to a series of tests.

How can I intimate this to my most intimate friend?

How Many Sounds Does OUGH make?

Pose that question to a group of older students at the beginning of the week and have them collect examples all week long. Then introduce this little nonsense sentence that follows. (Don't show them the *ough* sentence until they work with the question and do a thorough inquiry of it for several days.) Once they have done their inquiry, I tell them that the combination *ough* can be pronounced in nine different ways (which always surprises them). And then I read them this sentence, which contains all nine ways: "A rough-coated, dough-faced, thoughtful ploughman strode through the streets of Scarborough; after falling into a slough, he coughed and hiccoughed."

Appendix M
Children's Literature to Support Word Study

This is by no means an exhaustive list but does include a few of the best titles to get you started. It's important to tie your word study to real literature. Books about words can be difficult to find, but once you start looking you'll discover many out there. I devote a section in my class library to these books.

Miss Alaineus
by Debra Frasier

Sage ("one who shows wisdom, experience, judgment") is home sick and misunderstands one of Mrs. Page's vocabulary words for a homework assignment. She is very embarrassed in front of her fifth-grade class when she gets it all wrong. Somehow Sage thinks in her "defective and delirious" mind that Miss Alaineus is, "the woman on green spaghetti boxes whose hair is the color of uncooked pasta and turns into spaghetti at the ends." Sage walks away with the important lesson that "There's gold in every mistake." One sentence using vocabulary words from A to Z runs along the bottom or side of each page.

What in the World Is a Homophone?
If you don't know (no), then look inside to see (sea)!
by Leslie Presson

This book will make a great addition to your word study library. It is a colorful picture dictionary listing 387 sets of homophones. A nice addition is the inclusion of contractions that are homophones (*I'll, aisle, isle*) and near misses (*accept, except*). (Grades 1–5)

Frindle
by Andrew Clements

Nicholas is a bright boy who likes to make trouble at school, creatively. When he decides to torment his fifth-grade English teacher, Mrs. Granger (who is just as smart as he is), by getting everyone in the class to replace the word "pen" with "frindle," he unleashes a series of events that rapidly spins out of control. If there's any justice in the world, Clements (*Temple Cat*, etc.) may have something of a classic on his hands. By turns amusing and adroit, this first novel is also utterly satisfying. The chesslike sparring between the gifted Nicholas and his crafty teacher is enthralling, while Mrs. Granger is that rarest of the breed: a teacher the children fear and complain about for the school year and love and respect forever after. With comically realistic black-and-white illustrations by Selznick (*The Robot King*, etc.), this is a captivating tale—one to press upon children, and one they'll be passing among themselves. (Fiction, ages 8–12) *Copyright ©1996, Kirkus Associates, LP.*

C D B!
by William Steig

William Steig—*The New Yorker* cartoonist and revered author of dozens of other magnificent books—first wrote and illustrated the original, black-and-white edition of *C D B!* more than thirty years ago. Adding splashes of watercolor on larger, broader pages (and an answer key in the back!), Steig brings new life to his well-loved favorite. For the uninitiated, "C D B!" translates to "See the bee!" Other letter codes are more challenging, such as the boy leaning on a tree saying "I F-N N-E N-R-G" or a droopy, decrepit man slouching in a chair labeled "O-L H." Once you get used to this abbreviated Steig-speak, all (or at least most) will become clear—"X" sometimes means "eggs," "D" is sometimes "the," and "S" can be "is" or "has," for example. Or, you can just read the letters out loud over and over until the proper phrase emerges plain as day. (The pictures help, too, of course!) This book is nothing less than X-L-N, and no home where words are celebrated should be without it. (Ages 5 to 105) (Review from Amazon.com)

Abby Cadabra, Super Speller
by All Aboard Reading

Abby Cadabra is the best speller at the Hoakus Croakus School—that is until the arrival of a new student and equally talented speller, Wanda Cassandra. The competition between the two little witches is fierce, leading right up to the day of the big spelling bee. Not until then do they realize that F-R-I-E-N-D-S-H-I-P is the best "spell" of all. This is an All Aboard Reading Level Two book. (Review from Amazon.com)

Phoebe and the Spelling Bee
by Barney Saltzberg

After lying to her friend Katie about not studying for a spelling bee, Phoebe feels terrible and decides to study after all. Although she does not win the spelling bee, she is rewarded for the clever stories she makes up to remember words. The cheerful, childlike drawings help portray Phoebe as a spunky, likable character. *Copyright © 1998 The Horn Book, Inc. All rights reserved.*

Pinky and Rex and the Spelling Bee
by James Howe

Rex is a terrible speller, and she's afraid she's going to embarrass herself in front of the whole class at today's spelling bee. Pinky, on the other hand, is a great speller, and he's sure he's going to be champion of the second grade again. But Pinky isn't counting on the new kid in class, who's a great speller, too. And he's certainly not counting on embarrassing himself in a way so terrible that winning or losing doesn't even matter. It's a good thing he can count on Rex to make him feel better on the worst day of his life. (Review from Amazon.com)

(If you haven't tried the Pinky and Rex series they are excellent for beginning chapter book readers. My second graders *loved* this series. I always had to buy more because they were read over and over until they fell apart. There are six titles in the series by James Howe, who is also the author of *Bunnicula*.)

The Letters Are Lost
by Lisa Campbell Ernst

The premise of this alphabet book by Lisa Ernst is that the wooden blocks, with one letter to a block, were once together in their box. But now they've all gone astray. Where are they? Well, the A is in an airplane, the B has tumbled into the bath, and the L has landed in a pile of leaves. Each block is prominently featured in the framed paintings that show simple shapes and situations, which are, for the most part, easily identifiable to young ones. Although there is nothing especially groundbreaking about her book, Ernst gets high marks for having everything just right: the colors, the size, the appeal. At the book's conclusion, the blocks are back together but "not for long. Soon they will disappear again. Can you guess where they might go?" An open invitation to have children make up their own scenarios while learning their letters. Fun! (Review from *Booklist*)

Alphabet Soup
by Kate Banks and Peter Sis

A boy's ability to spell words with his alphabet soup comes in handy during the magical journey he takes in his mind with a friendly bear.

The Alphabet Tree
by Leo Lionni

Illustrated in full color. The letters on an alphabet tree, torn and tossed by the wind, find strength in banding together to form words. Then a clever caterpillar teaches the letters to become even stronger by forming sentences with a message of peace in a gentle parable about the power of the written word. (Review from Amazon.com)

Alphabetical Order
by Tiphaine Simoyault

Who invented the alphabet? How many different alphabets are there? Why do people need to write? All of these questions are discussed in *Alphabetical Order: How the Alphabet Began*. With full-color charts and illustrations showing exactly how signs and symbols evolved into letters and words, *Alphabetical Order* is a chance to see and understand the story behind the different alphabets people use every day. Tiphaine Samoyault is a professor of literature near Paris, where she makes her home. (Ages 9–12) (Review from Amazon.com)

The Disappearing Alphabet
by Richard Wilbur

This collection of 26 poems is definitely suited for the older reader. They'll enjoy Wilbur's wordplay as he wonders what it would be like in a world in which the alphabet begins to fade away. The cows would eat *hy* instead of hay, and serpents and snakes become hiss-less *erpents* and *nakes*. This sophisticated word play will spark many conversations during your word-crafting time.

The War Between the Vowels and the Consonants
by Priscilla Turner

A book for older students that takes a very clever look at what would happen if we didn't have vowels. In this imaginary world in which the vowels fight against the consonants, they learn that they need each other.

Word Wizard
by Cathryn Falwell

Another excellent books that shows what happens when we get intrigued by words. We start noticing them everywhere. Anna discovers that while eating her alphabet cereal at breakfast, she can rearrange the letters to make new words, thus making her a word wizard. Just what we want our students to become!

Ook the Book
by Lissa Rovetch

"I am Ook, Ook the book. Will you stop and take a look? You will see, I'm one good book!" What a perfect book to use to go along with your word families. There are twelve different characters including Ug the Bug, Ing the Thing, and In the Twin. The fun tongue-twisters are engaging and give students plenty of opportunities to engage in looking for common patterns.

There's an Ant in Anthony
by Bernard Most

Once Anthony realizes that he has a word (*ant*) in his name, he begins searching for the word in other words. He does exactly what we want our students to do with words. He is intrigued and becomes a word collector. You can even use this book to play with names of other students ("there's an *end* in Brenda," for example).

The Weighty Word Book
by Paul M. Levitt

It's difficult to explain the clever, crafty approach to this uniquely organized alphabet book. The concept is to introduce one big vocabulary word (like *truculent*) for every letter of the alphabet. For each letter, there is a little story that ends in a one-line sentence that gives you a way for remembering the big vocabulary word. For example, the story that went with the word *truculent* ends with, "So, whenever you want to describe someone who is fierce, or cruel, or savage, remember the truck Hugh lent, and you will remember the word." I read one story a day to my class and was so surprised at how they remembered these twenty-six new words all year.

Antics!
by Catherine Hepworth

A clever and more advanced version of *There's an Ant in Anthony*. Older students will enjoy the higher-level words and illustrations. In this book, the words contain the syllable *ant,* as in brilli*ant* and jubil*ant*.

Donavan's Word Jar
by Mona Lisa DeGross

Donavan is fascinated by words. A true word collector like we want our students to become, he finds them everywhere on books, signs, even the backs of cereal boxes. He collects the words on slips of paper in a big glass jar. One day, when the jar is almost full, Donavan has a dilemma. How can he make room for new words? This is an excellent book to use at the beginning of the year to launch your year as word crafters. You will ignite the interest in words in a wonderful social context based on a fine piece of children's literature.

References

Adams, Marilyn Jager. 1990. *Beginning to Read: Thinking and Learning About Print*. Cambridge: Harvard University Press.

Allred, Ruel A. 1993. "Integrating Proven Spelling Content and Methods with Emerging Literacy Programs." *Reading Psychology* 14 (January–March): 15–31.

Bean, Wendy, and Chrystine Bouffler. 1987. *Spell by Writing*. Rozelle, Australia: Primary English Teaching Association.

Bear, Donald R., and Diane Barone. 1989. "Using Children's Spellings to Group for Word Study and Directed Reading in the Primary Classroom." *Reading Psychology* 10: 275–92.

Bear, Donald R., Marcia Invernizzi, Shane Templeton, and Francine Johnston. 1995. 1999 (2d ed.). 2003 (3d ed.). *Words Their Way: Word Study for Phonics, Vocabulary, and Spelling Instruction*. Englewood Cliffs, NJ: Prentice-Hall.

Bear, Donald R., and Shane Templeton. 1998. "Exploration in Developmental Spelling: Foundations for Learning and Teaching Phonics, Spelling, and Vocabulary." *The Reading Teacher* 52 (November).

Beers, James W., and Edmund H. Henderson. 1977. "A Study of Developing Orthographic Concepts Among First Grade Children." *Research in the Teaching of English* 11 (2): 133–48.

Bissex, Glenda. 1980. *Gyns at Wrk: A Child Learns to Write and Read*. Cambridge: Harvard University Press.

Bolton, Faye, and Diane Snowball. 1993a. *Ideas for Spelling*. Portsmouth, NH: Heinemann.

———. 1993b. *Teaching Spelling: A Practical Resource*. Portsmouth, NH: Heinemann.

———. 1999. *Spelling K–8: Planning and Teaching*. York, ME: Stenhouse.

Brown, Sheron. 2000. *All Sorts of Sorts: Word Sorts for Reinforcing Spelling and Phonetic Patterns*. San Diego, CA: Teaching Resource Center.

———. 2002. *All Sorts of Sorts 2: Word Sorts for Complex Spelling & Phonetic Pattern Reinforcement.* San Diego, CA: Teaching Resource Center.

———. 2003. *All Sorts of Sorts 3: Word Sorts for Vocabulary Development in the Content Areas.* San Diego, CA: Teaching Resource Center.

Buchanan, Ethel. 1989. *Spelling for Whole Language Classrooms.* Katonah, NY: Richard C. Owen.

Calkins, Lucy M. 1980. "When Children Want to Punctuate: Basic Skills Belong in Context." *Language Arts* 57: 567–73.

Cates, Ward Mitchell, and Susan C. Goodling. 1997. "The Relative Effectiveness of Learning Options in Multimedia Computer-Based Fifth-Grade Spelling Instruction." *Educational Technology Research and Development* 45 (2): 27–46.

Chomsky, Carol. 1970. "Reading, Writing, and Phonology." *Harvard Educational Review* 40 (2): 287–309.

Clarke, Linda K. 1988. "Invented Versus Traditional Spelling in First Graders' Writings: Effects on Learning to Spell and Read." *Research in the Teaching of English* 22: 281–309.

Cline, Judith D., and Thomas F. McLaughlin. 1993. "An Analysis of Two Peer Tutoring Models for Spelling Performance with At-Risk Elementary School Students." *Journal of Special Education* 17 (1): 1–18.

Coiner, John M. 1995. "Is Word Study the Best Approach to Spelling Instruction?" In *A Study in the Effectiveness of Word Study vs. a Traditional Approach to Spelling Instruction.* ERIC Document Reproduction Service ED382939.

Cramer, Ron L. 1998. *The Spelling Connection: Integrating Reading, Writing, and Spelling Instruction.* New York: Guilford Press.

Cramer, Ron L., and James Cipielewski. 1995. "Research in Action: A Study of Spelling Errors in 18,599 Written Compositions of Children in Grades 1–8." In *Spelling Research and Information: An Overview of Current Research and Practices.* Glenview, IL: Scott, Foresman.

Cunningham, Patricia M. 1995. *Phonics They Use: Words for Reading and Writing,* 2d ed. New York: HarperCollins College.

Davis, Zephaniah T. 1987. "Upper Grades Spelling Instruction: What Difference Does It Make?" *English Journal* (March): 100–101.

DiStefano, Phillip, and Joellen Killion. 1984. "Assessing Writing Skills Through a Process Approach." *English Education* 16 (4): 203–7.

Dolch, Edward W. 1936. "A Basic Sight Vocabulary." *The Elementary School Journal* 36: 456–60.

Downing, John, Robert M. Coughlin, and Gene Rich. 1986. "Children's Invented Spellings in the Classroom." *The Elementary School Journal* 86 (January): 295–303.

Elkonin, D. B. 1963. "The Psychology of Mastering the Elements of Reading." In *Educational Psychology in the U.S.S.R.*, edited by B. Simon and J. Simon, pp. 165–79. Palo Alto, CA: Stanford University Press.

Fountas, Irene C., and Gay Su Pinnell. 1998. *Word Matters: Teaching Phonics and Spelling in the Reading/Writing Class.* Portsmouth, NH: Heinemann.

Freppon, Penny A., and Karin L. Dahl. 1991. "Learning About Phonics in a Whole Language Classroom." *Language Arts* 68: 190–97.

Fresch, Mary Jo. 2001. "Journal Entries as a Window on Spelling Knowledge." *The Reading Teacher* 54 (February).

Fresch, Mary Jo, and Aileen W. Wheaton. 2002. *Teaching and Assessing Spelling: A Practical Approach That Strikes the Balance Between Whole-Group and Individualized Instruction.* New York: Scholastic.

Fulk, Barbara Mushinski. 1997. "Think While You Spell: A Cognitive Motivational Approach to Spelling Instruction." *Teaching Exceptional Children* 29 (March–April): 70–71.

Fulk, Barbara Mushinski, and Melissa Stormont-Spurgin. 1995. "Fourteen Spelling Strategies for Students with Learning Disabilities." *Intervention in School and Clinic* 31 (September): 16–20.

Ganske, Kathy. 2000. *Word Journeys.* New York: Guilford.

Garan, Elaine M. 2002. *Resisting Reading Mandates: How to Truimph with the Truth.* Portsmouth, NH: Heinemann.

Gentry, J. Richard. 1985. "You Can Analyze Developmental Spelling—And Here's How to Do It!" *Early Years K–8* (May): 1–4.

———. 1987. *Spel . . . Is a Four-Letter Word.* New York: Scholastic.

———. 1997. *My Kid Can't Spell.* Portsmouth, NH: Heinemann.

———. 2000. "A Retrospective on Invented Spelling and a Look Forward." *The Reading Teacher* 54 (3): 318–32.

Gentry, J. Richard, and Jean Wallace Gillet. 1993. *Teaching Kids to Spell.* Portsmouth, NH: Heinemann.

Gettinger, Maribeth. 1993a. "Effects of Error Correction on Third Graders' Spelling." *Journal of Educational Research* 87 (September–October): 39–45.

———. 1993b. "Effects of Invented Spelling and Direct Instruction on Spelling Performance of Second-Grade Boys." 1993. *Journal of Applied Behavior Analysis* 26 (Fall): 281–91.

Glazer, Susan Mandel. 1994. "A Meaningful Way to Assess Spelling." *Teaching Pre-K–8* 24 (April): 87–88.

Gleick, James. 2000. *Faster: The Acceleration of Just About Everything.* New York: Vintage.

Goswami, Usha. 1991. "Learning About Spelling Sequences: The Role of Onsets and Rimes in Analogies in Reading." *Child Development* 62: 1110–23.

Graves, Donald H. 1977. "Research Update: Spelling Texts and Structural Analysis Methods." *Language Arts* 54 (January): 86–90.

———. 1983. *Writing: Teachers and Children at Work.* Portsmouth, NH: Heinemann.

Griffith, Priscilla L., and Mary W. Olson. 1992. "Phonemic Awareness Helps Beginning Readers Break the Code." *The Reading Teacher* 45: 516–25.

Harp, Bill. 1988. "When the Principal Asks, 'Why Are Your Kids Giving Each Other Spelling Tests?'" *Reading Teacher* 41 (March): 702–4.

Henderson, Edmund H. 1990. *Teaching Spelling*, rev. ed. Boston: Houghton Mifflin.

Henry, Marcia K. 1994. "Integrating Decoding and Spelling Instruction for the Disabled Reader." *Reading and Writing Quarterly: Overcoming Learning Difficulties* 10 (April–June): 143–58.

Hillocks, George, Jr., and Michael W. Smith. 1991. "Grammar and Usage." In *Handbook of Research on Teaching the English Language Arts,* edited by James Flood, Julie M. Jensen, Diane Lapp, and James R. Squire, pp. 591–603. New York: Macmillan.

Hoffman, Stevie, and Nancy Knipping. 1988. "Spelling Revisited: The Child's Way." *Childhood Education,* June: 284–87.

Horn, Ernest. 1926. *A Basic Writing Vocabulary: 10,000 Frequently Used Words in Writing.* Monograph First Series, No. 4. Iowa City: The University of Iowa.

Horn, Thomas. 1946. "The Effect of the Corrected Test on Learning to Spell." Master's Thesis. The University of Iowa.

Invernizzi, Marcia A., Mary P. Abouzeid, and Janet W. Bloodgood. 1997. "Integrated Word Study: Spelling, Grammar, and Meaning in the Language Arts Classroom." *Language Arts* 74 (March): 185–92.

Invernizzi, Marcia A., Mary P. Abouzeid, and Tom Gill. 1994. "Using Students' Invented Spellings as a Guide for Spelling Instruction That Emphasizes Word Study." *The Elementary School Journal* 95 (November): 155–67.

James, William James. 1958. [1899]. *Talks to Teachers on Psychology and to Students on Some of Life's Ideals.* New York: Norton.

Johnston, Francine R. 2001. "Spelling Exceptions: Problems or Possibilities?" *The Reading Teacher* 54 (4): 372–78.

Krashen, Stephen D. 1991. "Is Spelling Acquired or Learned? A Reanalysis of Rice (1897) and Cornman (1902)." *ITL: Review of Applied Linguistics* 91–92: 1–49.

Laminack, Lester L., and Katie Wood. 1996. *Spelling in Use.* Urbana, IL: National Council of Teachers of English.

Lutz, Elaine. 1986. "Invented Spelling and Spelling Development." ERIC Document Reproduction Service ED272922.

Masterson, Julie J., and Kenn Apel. 2000. "Spelling Assessment: Charting a Path to Optimal Intervention." *Topics in Language Disorders* 20 (3): 50–65.

Mills, Heidi, Timothy O'Keefe, and Diane Stephens.1992. *Looking Closely: Exploring the Role of Phonics in One Whole Language Classroom.* Urbana, IL: National Council of Teachers of English.

Moats, Louisa C. 1995. *Spelling Development, Disability, and Instruction.* Timonium, MD: York Press.

Morris, Darrell, Laurie Nelson, and Jan Perney. 1986. "Exploring the Concept of 'Spelling Instructional Level' Through the Analysis of Error Types." *The Elementary School Journal* 87 (2): 181–200.

Moustafa, Margaret. 1996. "Reconceptualizing Phonics Instruction in a Balanced Approach to Reading." Unpublished manuscript, San Jose State University.

Needleman, Carla. 1993. *The Work of Craft.* New York: Kondansha America.

Nelson, Laurie. 1989. "Something Borrowed, Something New: Teaching Implications of Developmental Spelling Research." *Reading Psychology* 10: 255–74.

Phenix, Jo. 1996. *The Spelling Teacher's Book of Lists.* Markham, ON: Pembroke.

Powell, Debbie, and David Hornsby. 1993. *Learning Phonics and Spelling in a Whole Language Classroom.* New York: Scholastic.

Read, Charles. 1971. "Preschool Children's Knowledge of English Phonology." *Harvard Educational Review* 41: 1–34.

Routman, Regie. 1994. *Invitations: Changing as Teachers and Learners K–12.* Portsmouth, NH: Heinemann.

Schlagal, Robert. 1989. "Constancy and Change in Spelling Development." *Reading Psychology* 10 (3): 207–32.

Schlagal, Robert, and Woodrow R. Trathen. 1998. "American Spelling Instruction: What History Tells Us." *American Reading Forum* (Online Journal: http://www.fd.appstate.edu/arfonline/98_arfyearbook/volume98toc.htm#Schlagal).

Scott, Jill E. 1994. "Spelling for Readers and Writers." *The Reading Teacher* 48 (October): 188–90.

Shannon, Patrick. 2001. *iSHOP You Shop: Raising Questions About Reading Commodities.* Portsmouth, NH: Heinemann.

Simmons, Janice L. 1978. "The Relationship Between an Instructional Level in Spelling and the Instructional Level in Reading Among Elementary School Children." Doctoral Thesis, University of Northern Colorado.

Sitton, Rebecca. 1996. *Rebecca Sitton's Spelling Source Book.* Scottsdale, AZ: Egger.

Templeton, Shane. 1986. "Synthesis of Research on the Learning and Teaching of Spelling." *Educational Leadership* (March): 73–78.

———. 1991. "Teaching and Learning the English Spelling System: Reconceptualizing Method and Purpose." *Elementary School Journal* 92: 185–201.

Templeton, Shane, and Darrell Morris. 1999. "Questions Teachers Ask About Spelling." *Reading Research Quarterly* 34 (1): 102–12.

Timberlake, Pat. 1995. "Robin, Owl, Eeyore, and Nvntd Splling." *Young Children* 50 (March): 66–67.

Toch, Thomas. 1992. "Nu Waz for Kidz tu Lern Rdn, Rtn." *U.S. News and World Report*, 14 September: 75–76.

Treiman, Rebecca, Marie Cassar, and Andrea Zukowski. 1994. "What Types of Linguistic Information Do Children Use in Spelling? The Case of Flaps." *Child Development* 65 (October): 1318–37.

Tunnell, Michael O., and James S. Jacobs. 1989. "Using 'Real' Books: Research Findings on Literature Based Reading Instruction." *The Reading Teacher* 42: 470–77.

Vos Savant, Marilyn. 2000. *The Art of Spelling: The Madness and the Method, What Our Spelling Says About Us.* New York: W. W. Norton.

Vygotsky, L. S. 1978. *Mind in Society: The Development of Higher Psychological Processes.* Cambridge: Harvard University Press.

Wagstaff, Janiel M. *Phonics That Work! New Strategies for the Reading/Writing Classroom.* Jefferson City, MO: Scholastic Professional.

Watson, Alan J. 1988. "Developmental Spelling: A Word Categorizing Instructional Experiment." *Journal of Educational Research* 82 (November/December): 82–88.

Weaver, Connie. 1994. *Reading Process and Practice: From Socio-psycholinguistics to Whole Language.* Portsmouth, NH: Heinemann.

———. 1996. *Teaching Grammar in Context.* Portsmouth, NH: Heinemann-Boynton/Cook.

Wilde, Sandra. 1990. "A Proposal for a New Spelling Curriculum." *The Elementary School Journal* 90 (January): 275–89.

———. 1992. *You Kan Red This! Spelling and Punctuation for Whole Language Classrooms, K–6.* Portsmouth, NH: Heinemann.

———. 1997. *What's a Schwa Sound Anyway?* Portsmouth, NH: Heinemann.

Index

vos Savant, Marilyn, 9, 11, 75
Vygotsky, Lev, 46, 56

W

Weaver, Connie, 7
Website, 121
What's a Schwa Sound Anyway?, 103
Wilbur, Richard, 149
Wilde, Sandra, 7, 9, 24, 31, 103
   "A Speller's Bill of Rights," 31
Wood, Katie, 102
Word crafting, 18–19, 22–23, 38
   key elements of, 23
Word hunt, 72
Word Journeys, 39–40, 99
Word reference books, 103
Word sorts, 70–72, 84, 99–100
Word Stems: A Dictionary, 104

Word study games, 84
Word study notebooks/journals, 71–72,
   84, 105, 107
Words about words, 74
Words Their Way, 39–40, 53, 62, 70–71, 98
   annual conference, 84, 98
WordWorks: Exploring Language Play, 101
Workbooks. *See* Curriculum guides
Writing, 7–8, 16, 49–50, 89–90
Writing: Teachers and Children at Work, 50
www.spellingtools.com, 121

Y

You Kan Red This!, 103

Z

Zone of proximal development, 46, 56
Zutell, Jerry, 20